NEW MINDSET
NEW RESULTS

NEW MINDSET
NEW RESULTS

KERRY JOHNSON
MBA, PHD

MEDIA

MEDIA

Published by Gildan Media LLC
aka G&D Media
www.GandDmedia.com

FIRST EDITION 2019
FIRST PAPERBACK EDITION 2021

Front Cover design by David Rheinhardt of Pyrographx

Interior design by Meghan Day Healey of Story Horse, LLC

Library of Congress Cataloging-in-Publication Data is available upon request

ISBN: 978-1-7225-0538-7

10 9 8 7 6 5 4 3 2 1

To My First Grandchild, Cora Anne

"I hope you always have a Results-Focused Mindset your whole life. Your wonderful parents will prepare you for the great success you deserve. You were specially made by our Lord God. Your grandparents love you to the moon and back"

Contents

Why I Wrote New Mindset, New Results

I've been speaking at conferences, coaching top producers, and writing books and recording videos since 1981. In all the time, I have focused mainly on developing skill sets to help my audiences and clients dramatically increase their business. In fact I often guarantee that my clients will increase their business by 80% within eight weeks. I'm so confident in our techniques that I can make that warranty.

But I have to admit, 5 to 10% of my clients don't realize the benefit they wanted. Another 25% skyrocket their business and hit their goals. 65% gain enough benefit to make their effort worthwhile, but could have done better. What is it between these three groups? They were all taught the same skills. They all had excellent coaching. Except for the bottom 10%, most work hard but had variable results. It had to be something else. There had to be way of thinking, a kind of motivation that could propel any client to become wildly successful. The answer is a Results Focused Mindset.

Billy Beane, manager of the four time division champion, Oakland A's, had only one third the money that World Series champions New York Yankees had. Beane didn't have the resources, but did have a different mindset. Beane once said, "Change your thinking, change the game." Mindset is the framework that connects everything. It allows sales and management skills, self-discipline, and communication to operate effectively. Without A Results Focused Mindset, all these skills will be disjointed. A Results Focused Mindset helps all your knowledge, skills and experience work together.

In this book, you will learn about many different kinds of mindsets. Fixed Versus Growth, Inward versus Outward, and even External versus Internal mindsets. But it's not enough to understand what mindsets are. The focus of this book is to Help You Develop a Results Focused Mindset. This is a mindset that will help you not just be more positive, but also achieve your goals.

THE UNIQUE FORMAT OF NEW MINDSET, NEW RESULTS

My friend Brian Tracy once said, "Leaders are readers." In fact, if you want to be among the 1% of top income earners, you'll read one book every month. If you read one book every week, not only will you become among the top 1% in income, but also be the most educated.

The problem is, most people don't read books, not even on their devices. But they do read magazine articles, watch videos, and listen to audio. I tried to write this book in the way you are most likely to read it.

Decades ago, I was a pro tennis player. I still play tennis four days a week, as well as play golf, scuba dive and snow ski around the world. You will read a lot of stories from my experiences relevant to the concepts I discuss. This style of writing will help you develop a new, more effective mindset. One San Diego State University study showed your memory of an idea will increase by 83% if the story is attached to what you're trying to remember.

WHY MINDSET IS SO SIGNIFICANT

This is my 9th book, and most important. Among these many books are: *Willpower: The Secrets of Self-Discipline*, *Peak Performance: How to Increase Your Business by 80% within Eight Weeks*, and even *Mastering the Game*. All have been wildly successful. But had I known how important an effective mindset was, my first book would have been different.

Your mindset is critical. It affects how you talk, your outlook, and even your happiness. It impacts how positive and negative you are, whether you are charismatic or shy, and is even an indicator of how much money will make over your career.

I was educated as a research psychologist. I was headed for academic or medical school becoming a psychiatrist. But after my MBA, I turned into a business psychologist. I have studied the actual peer-reviewed research of all the concepts you will read in this book. From my research background, I can outline what is meaningful from the actual recent study instead of just quoting a speaker or magazine article that alludes to the conclusions. In graduate school, I developed test predictors of stress symptoms for the Veterans Administration, how the brain differentiates food preferences for Continental/United Airlines, and even studied advanced body language techniques for vocational colleges. But the most surprising aspect I learned in writing this book was how much mindset changes the brain. I spent two years studying psychobiology of the brain. But the advancements since my research days have been remarkable. Mindset not only creates neural pathways, but also creates dense forest-like networks that solidify the mindset you have developed. In other words, the more you access a successful Results Focused Mindset, the easier it will be to sustain and maintain it. Our brains are built for worry and rumination. It's easier and more natural to think negatively than positively. But that is why mindset is so important. Highly successful people have a different way of thinking. They don't let themselves get bogged down with worry or paralyzed with negativity. They are able to sustain results focused mindset consistently.

This book will help you learn what an effective mindset is. But it doesn't stop there. It will also help you modify and change the mindset you have, developing one that will consistently help you achieve your dreams. I speak at many conventions every week around the world. I often surprise audiences by saying they will forget 70% of what I say within one day and 90% within three days. Unless they implement an idea within 24 hours of hearing it. This applies to you. If you can test out and use a concept within 24 hours, it is likely that you will retain it. So my goal is to not only help you change your mindset, but also sustain that mindset for years to come.

Please read this book and let me know what you think. Contact me at:

www.KerryJohnson.com

Kerry@KerryJohnson.com

714-368-3650

Twitter@DrKerryJohnson

LinkedInKerry Johnson, MBA, PhD

1

Why Is Mindset So Important?

In 1991, PGA Tour officials phoned a young golfer from Dardanelle, Arkansas, asking if he could be the ninth alternate at Crooked Stick Golf Club in Carmel, Indiana, for the PGA championship. Unfortunately, the young golfer was unlikely to play. The day before the first round, he set his cruise control to seventy and drove the 670 miles to Carmel, arriving at 2 a.m. But destiny arrived when tour officials informed him on the way to the tournament that in fact he would play. His tee time was only hours after his arrival.

Nobody expected this loud, brash, unsophisticated, player who hit 350-yard tee shots to win. But John Daly won the tournament three strokes ahead of Bruce Lietzke. (You could say that lightning, figuratively speaking, struck Daly. But lightning literally struck spectator Thomas Weaver, who was killed from a lightning strike on the first day.) Media and pros alike had never seen a swing like Daly's.

As soon as he could read, Daly had been given a golf instructional guide written by Jack Nicklaus. John modeled his swing after his hero's. Nicklaus coincidentally said, "Daly's stroke isn't like mine. It is unlike anything I've ever seen."

But John Daly had a mindset. He had a belief in himself and way of thinking that was different. That unique pattern of thoughts would create a champion. John Daly simply said, "I only think about one thing when I swing. I grip it and rip it." Daly's attitude was to always swing hard. If he won, he won big. If he lost, he lost big. His only other major golf tournament win was the British Open in 1995, when he defeated Costantino Rocca in a playoff. But what helped him win was a winning mindset—a thought pattern that helped him get results. It helped him win twenty-two professional tournaments.

Mindset is a mental inclination: a frame of mind. Your mindset filters how you see the world. It's how you make sense of everything that affects you. It also enables you to evaluate people, concepts, objects, and events with consistency. Your mindset is a compilation of your thoughts and beliefs, which create habits. Habits in turn affect how you think, what you feel, and what you do.

You can also think of mindset as an attitude. Psychologists say that an attitude is a learned tendency to see things in a certain way. It is a consistent way we feel about people and things.

There are three components of mindset:

1. An emotional component: how a person, object, or event makes you feel

2. A cognitive component: your thoughts, beliefs, and expectations

3. A behavioral component: how your mindset affects your behavior

There are three basic building blocks of mindset.

1. You create beliefs.

2. Your beliefs shape your attitude.

3. Your attitude and beliefs create your mindset.

It's almost as though mindset is a chair. It supports you with the legs of ideas, beliefs, expectations, and attitudes. If you take out a leg, the chair's support becomes more unstable. Similarly, a negative expectation will weaken the support that mindset gives you.

One of my daughter Catherine's friends, Greg, dropped out of the University of Colorado to enlist in the Marines. I live in Southern California and was able to see Greg every few months during his leaves from basic training. When I knew him in Boulder, Colorado, he had been a hard-drinking, undirected member of a college party gang. But his transformation was remarkable.

Every Marine will tell you that basic-training instructors start by immediately ripping apart every belief, concept, and idea you have. They will berate you from the first day, challenging your family, education, relationships, and even your goals—all of this in an attempt to develop a good Marine. Why are the instructors so deprecating and insulting of their recruits? They have the goal of tearing down every mindset those young recruits have. Then they create another mindset, one that's consistent with the Marine's goals of completing a mission and achieving success in any situation. Marines have a mindset of taking lawful orders and achieving their goals within the rules and guidelines established by the Marine Corps. Marines don't create individuals; they create teams that work together and complete missions.

WHAT IS YOUR MINDSET?

What are your beliefs? What are your expectations? Take this short quiz to determine your mindset. I will give you some definitions of mindset, each accompanied by a question that will illustrate your own.

1. A mindset is a mental attitude that predetermines your responses to people in any situation.

Do you walk into a meeting with apprehension, or positive expectation? Do you meet people with the mindset of opportunity, or do you feel they might judge you?

2. Your mindset influences your tendencies, inclinations, and habits.

Do you wake up in the morning and immediately do your workout, or do you ruminate and worry? Do you look at your day wondering what you will accomplish, or do you focus on the obstacles you will face?

3. Your mindset is your attitude and mental state.

Is your day one of positive attitude, or do you wonder what negative things may happen to you?

4. Your thinking and opinions are guided by your mindset.

Is your thinking directed toward building something and growing who you are, or is it about protecting yourself and what you have? Are your opinions open, or are you polarized, like today's U.S. political parties?

5. Your mindset is also your mood and disposition.

Is your mood uplifting. looking for reasons for encouragement, or do you blame others and your surroundings for your results?

6. Your mindset is how you approach a situation—especially when it could cause you stress.

If a situation in the past has caused you stress, do you avoid it, or do you look for ways to change your past results?

How did you score on this mindset quiz? This was meant to show you that who you are, how you think, and what you do is directed by your mindset. All your good habits of smiling when you meet people, getting to work on time, and providing for your family are the results of your mindset. All your bad habits of procrastination, not working out enough, and overeating are also influenced by your mindset.

I have a friend who tells me that he is rarely late. He says if you're not early, you're late. There's no on-time. I asked him where he learned this concept. He said, "That's just the way I think." This is mindset directing his attitude, thoughts, and behavior.

WHAT YOU WILL GAIN FROM THIS BOOK

In this book, we will discuss many areas that can dramatically improve your life. Your mindset affects everything you do think, say, and experience. We will talk about why your mindset is so important, and will give you a sense of what your mindset is right now. We will talk about where it came from and how it influences, impacts, and even biases everything you experience. We will also talk about the differences between *inward* and *outward* mindset. Inward-mindset people think solely about themselves, while outward-mindset people consider the impact of their behavior on other people.

Most of the research on this subject has come from Stanford professor Carol Dweck, who divided the category into *fixed mindset* and *growth mindset*. Fixed-mindset people think of their talents and abilities as limited. Growth-mindset people think of their success as being dependent mainly on their effort. They look at setbacks not as limiting, but as learning experiences they can use to overcome similar obstacles later.

You will also learn in this book that your IQ is not baked in. It is just the measurement of a moment in time of your ability to learn. It is critically important to know that your IQ now doesn't limit who you can be. It is only an indication of your ability right now.

From all this research, I will help you develop a new mindset, one that is focused on results. I will help you develop a mindset you can use, not to limit yourself, but to create a new way of thinking—a mindset built on the belief that you can create anything you want. I will help you build a new Results-Focused Mindset. I will help you recast how you perceive and think. Through *content* and *context recasting,* I will help you change your emotions, behaviors, and memories into those that support the mindset you want.

You see the world from your own frame of reference. It's hard to ask a fish the temperature of the water when that is where it lives. It has nothing to compare it to. It's also hard to change your mindset without helping you change the beliefs that don't support the mindset you want. But this will be easy if you apply my suggestions for creating change. Some of the self-limiting beliefs you have are learned. You have even learned how to fail. The causes include learned helplessness, a high level of sensitivity to criticism, and as you age, a resistance to learning.

But you will also receive great tips on how to develop a new Results-Focused Mindset. You will learn how to strengthen your mindset through techniques like a *resource circle,* changing how you think through *meta-patterns,* and using *slicing and outcomes* in creating and achieving goals.

Have you ever been distracted from making life changes? Have you ever created New Year's resolutions that lasted only a few weeks? Well, I'm like you. I need specific strategies that I can use to keep from procrastinating and, sometimes, from getting discouraged. Because of this, I'm going to help you develop a *behavioral contract* in building your new Results-Focused Mindset. We are even going to create rewards you can give yourself for staying faithful to your daily agreement. Your mindset also impacts your brain. This applies to not only how you think, but your mindset actually changes your brain structures. In fact, the more you worry, the more you physically change your brain, making it become more negative. Your brain pathways become like freeways of worry, causing you to ruminate even more. To combat this, we will apply a couple of techniques including *pattern interrupt*, substituting negative thoughts for a positive mindset, and reminding yourself consistently to check on whether your thoughts support the mindset you want.

We will also talk a lot about the mindset of great leaders. We will discuss how they think, not only they themselves, but the people they develop. We will focus on some specific mindset skills you can develop, including negotiation.

Lastly, we will talk about how to develop a better mindset in others. You can actually help your children create a great mindset. But it won't be through praising how great they are; instead it will be focused on encouraging their effort. This will help them develop a love for achievement through effort, instead of expecting success because of who they are.

We will also see how we can develop this new Results-Focused Mindset in others through *successive approximation* and *behavior shaping*. As we'll see, SeaWorld uses these same techniques used to create amazing feats with killer whales, otters, and seals.

Finally, we will talk about how your talent and ability have very little to do with your success. With your new Results-Focused Mindset, you will be able to overcome obstacles more effectively, and see setbacks simply as learning experiences. We will also talk about the mindset of arrogance and narcissism. Many countries have had a collective mindset of thinking they were better than others. Because of their mistaken sense of superiority, they have all collapsed.

DEVELOPING A SELF-CONFIDENT MINDSET

According to Dr. Ivan Joseph, athletic director and soccer coach at Ryerson University, mindset is a key component he uses in selecting soccer players for scholarships. Joseph says that parents will approach him and talk about their kids. They will say, "My child has great vision." Or they will say, "My child is able to see the whole field better than any other kid out there." Or, "My child has a left foot strike better than anybody at his school."

But what Joseph looks for most is not their soccer skill set, but their mindset about hard work and effort. Can these recruits learn? He tries to spot the students who have belief in themselves. He looks for players who never lose sight of their goals and will strive to win, no matter what the odds.

Joseph describes a few things you can do to build a solid success-focused mindset. These are simple yet effective techniques you can use to develop a mindset that creates self-confidence. He is not talking about irrational self-confidence, whereby you act as if you have a skill that you don't have. (I love the insurance commercial that shows a man who is so confident after buying insurance that he goes to a street performer juggling three chainsaws and says, "Give me a chance, I know I can do this.") No, we're not talking about irrational confidence when a skill is needed and you possess none. We are talking about ways to build a mindset possessing self-confidence in anything that you do.

In the first place, according to Joseph, in order to build a mindset of self-confidence, you need *repetition*. Author Malcolm Gladwell discusses the 10,000-hour rule: if you do anything for 10,000 hours, you'll become an expert. Joseph tells the story of a goalie he recruited from South America. While the goalie had good feet, his hands were like stone. No matter what was thrown, he would drop it. So Joseph made the goalie catch 350 soccer balls at the goal net, every day, for eight months. The goalie with stone hands is now playing pro soccer in Europe, at the highest levels.

Many people might be willing to catch 350 balls a day, but not for eight months. Most people won't practice anything for 10,000 hours. They'll quit when it gets tough. They'll bail out when they get bored. They won't put in the hard yards to get the things they want. J.K. Rowling was rejected thirteen times by publishers before she was able to convince one to publish the *Harry Potter* series. But because of her great persistence, Rowling became the first billion-dollar author the world had ever seen. As you have undoubtedly heard, Edison tried 10,000 light bulbs before one worked. He was known to say that with each mistake, he narrowed it down one more.

The CNBC show *Blue-Collar Millionaire* recently featured a young woman grossing $20 million a year by breeding horses. Her father had told her, "You can't make money by breeding horses." Her secret was ability to find great mares with great genes. But it wasn't really about ability. It was all about hard work. She came from a rodeo family, but she was the first to make money with the animals she loved.

Two college graduates were both in jobs they hated. After three years, they wanted a change. Borrowing a parent's van, they hauled junk away for a small fee. These young entrepreneurs built a franchise grossing $25 million a year, just hauling junk. Living in Miami, one has a house on the inland waterway, while the other owns a Maserati. Both are married now with young kids. If you asked if they were smart, they would say yes. If you asked if they were lucky, they would say, "Of course." But if you asked if they were lazy, both would say no. It was all about effort; it was all about hard work.

One of my favorite blue-collar millionaires is a pest exterminator from Atlanta, Georgia. He bought his father's company for $5 million and built it into an $8 million enterprise in just a few years. With a very low overhead of only 40 percent, and an income of $8 million, this is successful, no matter what you do. But the interesting part about making $8 million as a pest-control expert is what he has to put up with. Searching an attic for two-day-dead rats will make anyone throw up. Breaking open walls to find nests of termites and cockroaches is more than enough.

But the real success story for these four blue-collar millionaires is not only about hard work. Each of them independently said, "There is no quit in them." Eighty-five percent of entrepreneurs will fail in their first three years. Why? Is it because of cash flow? Is it because of a lack of advertising? It's more because of their mindset. I think it's more about their inability to overcome obstacles. It's their lack of effort in dealing with setbacks.

Second, people with a mindset of self-confidence have *uplifting self-talk*. Many of us talk to ourselves negatively. We'll say things like, "I hope I don't mess this up. I hope I don't make that mistake again. I can't believe how stupid I am." My sister-in-law told us recently that she spent the whole night worrying whether she would screw up the family's prime-rib Christmas dinner. She did her homework and was totally prepared. Yet she still worried.

Self-talk sets the stage for mindset. How you talk to yourself is a reflection of your mindset. How you talk is how you behave. Your mind doesn't filter how you talk to yourself. If it's negative, you will act out those thoughts. If it's positive, your behavior will be consistent with that as well.

Self-talk is a little like the baseball pitcher who says to himself, "Don't throw high and inside on this batter." Sure enough, on the next pitch, the ball is thrown high and inside, exactly what the pitcher did *not* want to do. The mind has a difficult time distinguishing negative self-talk from positive self-talk. Your thoughts are a reflection of your self-talk. In other words, if you talk to yourself negatively, negative things happen. If you talk to yourself positively, positive things happen.

In middle of a tennis match many years ago, I double-faulted on a key point. I berated myself. I actually said out loud, "What a stupid shot. I have to be the worst tennis player at this club." Sure enough, I lost the match because I played even worse on the next points. This was a result of my negative self-talk. That's why athletes have to have a kind of amnesia. They have to totally forget their past mistakes, thinking only about the sure success of the next point.

Third, Joseph says you should *get away from anybody who will tear you down*. I call this "The Theory of the Thousand Cuts." It's not the elephants that get you, it's the mosquitoes. If one person says you can't do something, maybe you can get over it. But if many people diminish your goals or ability, perhaps you start believing them.

Professional speakers like me are known for their healthy egos. A mindset of self-confidence is pretty important. Ever heard a shy speaker before? Not very inspiring! Audience rejection can be intense, especially when you are just starting out. I confided once that a seminar attendee gave me grief, saying my humor was sophomoric. One of my not-so-encouraging colleagues once said, "If someone calls you an ass, consider the source. When two people call you an ass, buy a saddle." It's good to get a dose of reality, but you don't want people around you who won't and don't support the mindset you are trying to develop.

Think about the people around you. Do they support your goals and abilities? Do they uplift you, or do they build themselves up by diminishing you? Here is one more question from a psychologist: can you tell the difference between the two types of people who do each?

Finally, Joseph says that a mindset of self-confidence includes an ability to *catalog your own past success*es. I remember my daughter Caroline playing tennis. I watched one of her matches and asked afterward, "How did you do?" She said, "I played great, Dad, I was really on today." Was she playing the same match that I saw? She had barely touched the ball. The other team hit to her partner 90 percent of the time. She hit a couple of good shots, but that was it. Caroline only remembered the good shots. Even so, her interpretation of how she played was everything.

If you are like me, I try to remember how I did the last time. But deeper than that, I tend to remember my mistakes more vividly than my successes. There is a theory among pro athletes that the pain of losing is worse than the joy of winning. My friend, Pittsburgh Steelers quarterback turned TV broadcaster Terry Bradshaw, heard me say this and then told me about all the pick-six interceptions he had thrown. Even though he was a four-time Super Bowl champion, he remembered the mistakes vividly.

People with a mindset of self-confidence will remember success more intensely than failure. They will catalog successful situations and try to forget the events they did poorly in. Or they will reinterpret and recharacterize those poor past events as simply learning experiences, helping them to become better. If you are a person who tends to remember poor performances instead of great ones, this could be difficult. But practice makes perfect. Catch yourself remembering your great successes and reward yourself for each step in the effort of gaining them. We will talk about how to reward yourself later, but if you make the effort to achieve, treat yourself to something special now. If you make a sale, go out to dinner the same day. If you are on schedule and complete the first day of a project, go get a cup of yogurt, like my daughter Catherine. If you clean the garage, take your wife out to dinner, even if you have more work to do tomorrow. Rewards can make memories of your successes more intense.

WHERE DID YOUR MINDSET COME FROM?

Like other behaviors, your mindset is a product of the feedback you have received from teachers, parents, friends, and even your coaches. A teacher who encourages you in math may be able to create a mindset that you can solve any problem. A parent who says that you are irresponsible may create a mindset that you can't be depended on. A coach who often says, "Don't miss" may cause you to doubt yourself, creating fear that you will miss in the future.

My heroes before I played on the pro tennis tour were Stan Smith, Rob Laver, and Jimmy Connors. Shortly after I retired from my brief career, John McEnroe came on the scene. The 1981 Wimbledon final between McEnroe and Bjorn Borg was arguably the best in tennis history. Borg had beaten McEnroe in the finals in 1980, creating an even better final the following year. But 1981 was the year of McEnroe's redemption. Nevertheless, John McEnroe was not brought up by his father to develop a winning mindset. McEnroe said his father pushed him too hard. Many tennis parents often take the fun out of game. John's father seemed to live for growing his son's junior career. John actually told his father that he was not enjoying tennis. He asked him, "Do you have to come to every practice?" John brought his father the success he wanted, but John didn't enjoy any part of it.

Later in his career, McEnroe said he loved the adulation, the money, and the fame. But he didn't truly love to play the sport. Contrast this to tennis champion Roger Federer. He has often told reporters that retirement would be the worst phase of his life, because he loves to play tennis so much. You can see his mindset even in the matches he loses. He is always congratulatory, praising his opponent. He doesn't talk about how badly he played, but instead about how good his opponent was. Most of all, he talks about how much he enjoyed the match. Roger Federer was number one in the world for 302 weeks. John McEnroe was number one in the world for only 170 weeks. The difference was that Roger Federer's mindset was one of enjoyment of the game. John McEnroe's mindset was only to please his father.

All of your childhood experiences have contributed to create your mindset. Later we will discuss how to change your mindset to what you want it to be.

HOW YOUR MINDSET INFLUENCES YOUR BIASES

As I mentioned before, mindset influences your emotions, thoughts, and behavior towards the world. We all have filters for evaluating the information that we process. If we acted on everything we heard and read, we would go nuts. Your mindset is a filter that causes you to create biases about the things you experience. It's kind of a chicken and egg concept. Your mindset influences your biases, and your biases support your mindset. Some of the many filtering biases that maintain your mindset include *herd behavior, status quo, recency* (what you most recently remember), *extremeness*, and *loss aversion*. One of the most powerful is called *confirmation bias*.

Confirmation bias is the tendency we have to look for, and be persuaded by, information that supports beliefs we have already accepted. In my book *Why Smart People Make Dumb Mistakes with Their Money*, I detailed the research of Cornell University marketing professor Ed Russo. He asked students to evaluate restaurants. He showed them photographs and menus and asked the students to rate the establishments from one to ten, one being low, ten being high. Some students liked the menu of a given restaurant and gave it a nine, while other students were less impressed and gave it a three. But then the students were taken inside the restaurant. They saw its less appealing aspects, such as torn cushions, messy floors, and the poor state of the restrooms. Russo then asked the students to rate the restaurant again. Even after the students had seen the restaurant, the ratings varied slightly from the initial scores by only 10 percent.

Companies depend on confirmation bias to build their brands. Bose headphones sound so good that when an "in-ear" model is introduced, your assumption will be that the Bose excellence will be maintained. When Porsche comes out with a hybrid, your bias is one of excellent engineering and performance. On the other hand, it takes a lifetime to get over a bad first impression. Your initial impression is hard to change.

A few years ago, I decided to go on a vacation to Belize with my family. We booked the airfare and hotel and couldn't wait to go. But a hurricane traveled through he Caribbean for three days before the trip. My wife wanted me to cancel, but I argued that the storm would miss Belize. I looked at its trajectory and the wind patterns and convinced myself that our vacation wasn't in jeopardy. It wasn't until the hotel called and said they were closing their property for five days that I relented. It wasn't that I didn't know a hurricane was going through the area. It was that I only listened to the news reports predicting the hurricane would pass north of Belize instead of through it.

Dick Winick, of Cornerstone Research in Boston, noticed when consumers select the same brand of car year after year, they pay more. Buick owners paid an average of $2500 more per vehicle, while Mercedes owners paid an average of $10,000 more. The reason for the high premium is that loyal owners tend to be less skeptical and less willing to negotiate than new buyers, who are more inclined to negotiate the right deal. You will always get a better deal if you are prepared to walk away. Confirmation bias is also supported by constantly improving technology. Cars don't break down as often and have longer warranties. Today you are less likely to be disappointed with your purchase.

Many years ago, I went to a BMW dealership looking to buy a new 650i. There were some beautiful cars on the lot. My wife, Merita, asked if I had ever driven a Porsche. (During seminars now I jokingly say, "Is it pronounced *Porsh* or *Porsha*? I am just curious, since I used to own a Toyot!") I came for a BMW but was curious about the 2003 Turbo on the far side of a lot. I test-drove it and was immediately converted into a Porsche fan. It was so fast, it flew below radar. I had owned four BMWs before that shopping trip, but I was now on a mission to buy a Porsche 911s Carrera. I was also a first-time Porsche buyer. Eventually I found a Carrera in Pasadena. I negotiated a $15,000 discount, unheard-of in most Porsche dealerships. The car had been on the lot for three months. I was totally willing to walk away unless I got the right price. I recently bought another Porsche, but didn't negotiate nearly as hard. I was in love with the brand. I didn't get the best deal. I had developed confirmation bias. So the next time you want to buy a car, don't be in love with the model or the make. Be willing to buy a car from a different manufacturer if you want to save money.

Whether it's a car, food, or vacation spots, once you have developed a confirmation bias, you will view new information through a filter that supports that bias. This is probably the reason I have never been able to get my daughters to listen to what I don't like about their boyfriends. They are sold on whomever they are attracted to, and disregard information that is inconsistent with their beliefs. (For the record, the boys they are with now are pretty nice. But fathers never think boys are good enough for their girls.)

One of my clients was in search of a new office assistant. He received twenty responses from an online ad. The applicant he liked best currently had a job. When she phoned, it was from her previous employer's office. I asked my client if he was bothered that the candidate was using company time to apply for a new job. He said, "I'm sure she won't do that when she works for me." A mindset of confirmation bias strikes again. Three months after, he terminated her because she was using office time to do personal business. As all my daughters and clients have often heard, "When people show you who they are, you should believe them."

After I got married in 1990, I gave a speech in Torquay, a seaside resort town in southwest England. We arrived in London, rented a car, and spent the night in Sussex. My wife, Merita, wanted to spend the afternoon antiquing. She found a beautiful grandfather clock. I thought it was way too expensive at $1000, but she was convinced it was a find, worth $3000 in the U.S. Back home, a dealer appraised it at only $500. My beautiful wife was the victim of confirmation bias. She was unwilling to listen to a conflicting viewpoint.

People often hear what they want to hear. They focus on information that confirms their beliefs and explains away any evidence and information that conflicts. As a result, many decisions are based on information that is inaccurate, incomplete, and/or simply wrong. Before the presidential election of 2008, late-night host Jay Leno did one of his man-on-the-street interviews in New York's Harlem district. He asked residents what they thought of Barack Obama. If they were willing to vote for Obama, Leno would then ask what they thought of his pro-life stance,and what they thought of his choice of Sarah Palin for his running mate. In nearly every case, respondents thought Obama was right in being pro-life and anti-abortion. They agreed that having a woman as his vice-presidential running mate was a terrific idea. Actually, the opposite was true. Obama is pro-choice, and his running mate was not Sarah Palin, it was Joe Biden. But because of confirmation bias, statements were accepted if they supported Obama or disregarded if they conflicted. By the way, confirmation bias also affects supporters of Donald Trump, Bill Clinton, and every other president who has ever served.

While overcoming confirmation bias is always difficult, there are ways you can mitigate it. First, get the opinion of at least two other sources before you make up your mind. (Of course, this may be easier said than done, since you will probably be biased quickly toward your favorite piece of advice.) Next, do your research. If you only have a hammer, you treat the whole world as if it's a nail. If you only have a little information, you will project your decision based on it. So look at good and bad information with equal weight. You may still make some mistakes, but at least now they will be more educated ones.

MINDSET AND CHANGE

According to a recent study by management consultants McKinsey and Company, organizations and companies that focus on changing mindsets are four times more successful in their change efforts than companies that neglect mindset.

I am a business psychologist. I've been speaking around the world for more than forty years. I have visited every continent in the world and nearly every country except Russia. In my travels speaking at conventions, I have seen companies make dramatic improvements. This is because they have first reformed their company's culture. Companies change compensation systems and incentives, and will even threaten negative consequences. But here lasting changes are rare. Why? Because they are trying to change behavior, not mindset. We know that behavior drives results. But mindset drives behavior.

Often I'm hired to deliver motivational speeches to pump up employees in an organization. Usually I'm the last resort after senior executives have failed at every other strategy. Many years ago, I was the after-dinner speaker at an executive placement company. There were a hundred associates in attendance, and they were getting drunker by the minute. The senior vice-president got up to introduce me. He told the group, "I want you all to know that we have cut your commissions, decreased your salary by 10 percent, and increased your medical co-pay by $500 a month. And I'd like to introduce our keynote speaker, Dr. Kerry Johnson, to motivate you all to even higher achievements and give you a big sendoff." Needless to say, I did not get a standing ovation that evening. It's like the bumper sticker that says, "Beatings will stop once performance improves."

2

The Outward, Growth, and Fixed Mindsets

According to James Farrell's book *The Outward Mindset: Seeing Past Ourselves*, people and organizations can make lasting changes only if they have an outward mindset. An outward mindset means that you are aware of and interested first in the needs of other people rather than your own. Those with an inward mindset are focused only on their own objectives and their own narrow responsibilities. They are often focused more on the process of what they do than on how it affects the organization. This may also apply to you individually. Do you do things with yourself in mind, or do you focus on how it might affect your family and friends?

I played tennis a few months ago with a group of four good friends. As we often do after a match, we shared a pitcher of beer. One friend said his wife wanted him home by 6 p.m. for dinner. At 7, I said, "Too late—I think your wife will not be happy." He said, "I'm not worried; she will only get mad for a while." This is an example of an inward mindset: thinking more about what you want instead of the people affected by your behavior.

In my practice, I often find employee silos within companies.

These are people with set job processes and responsibilities who resent those who affect them. This could be an administration person who feels threatened when another assistant is hired. It could be a salesperson who resents another salesperson joining the team. Or it could be those upset by a corporate reorganization that changes job responsibilities.

Many years ago I had a very sharp salesperson leave me for another speaker. She told me that the speaker, whom I knew very well, offered to pay her 25 percent more money. But when someone says they are leaving the company for more money, it's usually a cover-up for something else. I also had an administrative person who was only focused on her accounting, event planning, and office systems. She was seemingly uninterested in whether my company was growing or declining. She was only interested in her systems.

The salesperson was admittedly very lax in detail. She rarely produced paperwork backing up the speeches she booked, and almost never produced written reports for her weekly activity, although all that was required. But she was such a great salesperson that I usually produced the paperwork for her. The administrative person, on the other hand, was so focused on her systems and processes that she became passive-aggressive, irritating everybody else. The salesperson quit for my competitor as a result.

In *The Outward Mindset*, Farrell discusses some mindset patterns that you can apply.

1. **Seeing Others.** This means becoming curious about and focused on the needs, obstacles, and objectives of those you interact with. Leaders will create opportunities for people to grow. They will help their subordinates overcome obstacles to make them more successful. Coworkers can do things in a way that helps others succeed.

One of my coaching clients is a family business. The chief is a financial adviser with three associates and four administrators. His wife heads the administrative side. The biggest-producing associate routinely produces paperwork with errors, if he turns them in at all. This creates enormous work for the wife, who then has to spend hours calling clients and dealing with compliance staff, wasting hours of her time. All this could be headed off if only the associate had an outward mindset instead of an inward focus.

2. **Adjust Efforts**. Developing an understanding of what other people around you are trying to accomplish. Are you doing things to make your own efforts helpful to the people you interact with? The interesting thing is that as you help other people, they will also help you accomplish your goals.

3. **Focus on Impact.** Inward-mindset people focus on what they do. Outward-mindset people focus on the impact of what they do *on others*. People with an outward mindset say they feel accountable for their impact.

One way to have enormous impact is to speak to a group. It is also usually terrifying. One of the biggest fears people have is speaking in front of a group. I was in Las Vegas many years ago, delivering a speech to a thousand business owners on "How to Read Your Customer's Mind." These business owners were often requested to speak in front of groups, so the speaker after me spoke about becoming a better speaker. He said, "There are three big fears people have in life. Number one, peaking in front of a group. Number two, dying. And number three, presumably, is dying while speaking in front of a group." I'm a pretty entertaining speaker. But when I heard this great line I convulsed with laughter.

The reason that people are so terrified of speaking is they are inwardly focused. They are totally consumed with how they are going to feel, how well they will do, and whether people will like them.

Contrast this with the most effective speakers I've ever heard, who also have been among my best friends. These are motivational greats: Cavett Robert, Charlie "Tremendous" Jones, Zig Zigler, Roger Dawson, and Les Brown. During their speeches, every one of these brilliant speakers is completely focused on the impact they have on the audience. Can they change people's lives? Can they help people improve? When you have an outward mindset with a group, the anxiety and fear dissipate as your desire to make an impact takes over. If you really want to become a great speaker, develop an outward mindset and focus on what you do can do for your audience. As Norman Vincent Peale once said, "If you can help people get what they want, they will help you get what you want."

One of the toughest and most physically demanding training programs in the world is the Basic Underwater Demolition School (BUDS) SEAL team training. Not only do the SEALs only accept the best in the Navy, but they also encourage candidates to drop out—the sooner the better. The reasoning is this: if a candidate quits in BUDS training, they will also quit during a mission. Captain Rob Newson, a career Navy SEAL, reports that candidates can quit whenever they want by ringing a bell that hangs at the side of the Coronado or Virginia Beach BUDS training compounds. Newson says that every candidate who quits first begins with an inward mindset. They stop thinking about their teammates and mission and focus only on themselves. But as long as candidates thought only of the mission and of the people around them, they could get through anything. And the word *anything* has deep meaning. These candidates are sleep-deprived for a week, wet, cold, and bone-tired. The single biggest indicator of whether these select few will make it through the hardest military training in the world is *mindset*—not ability, not strength, just mindset.

Another example of an outward mindset is focusing on something much larger than yourself. Christian evangelists often talk about forgoing successful business careers for the joy of saving souls and ministering to their congregations. Whenever you hear of a soldier falling on a grenade, risking his life for his buddy, it is because he is focusing on the sacrifice for a bigger cause.

One of my coaching clients runs a successful insurance agency. Richard is gifted in his sales skills and even has an email handle called "The Greatest Closer." He easily qualifies for the top of the Million Dollar Round Table, which requires you to have a minimum of $1 million a year in income. But his success does not come from his sale skills or his persistence. His greatest gift is his passion and belief that his prospects need life insurance to protect their families, have a source of retirement income, and benefit from long-term care, as well as accumulating retirement savings tax-free. He truly cares less about how much money he makes—although that is important—than about his clients' well-being. He is flat-out passionate about making sure that people's lives are bettered by what he sells. I have coached one-on-one with hundreds of clients. Perhaps 5 percent of these people have Richard's passion about helping their clients. The funny thing is, the more of an outward mindset my clients have, the more money they make.

One of my clients from Maine a few years ago was the opposite. Jim would often miss coaching appointments and would even more frequently make excuses for his low activity. After a few months, I realized he would only put in the effort to help his clients when he needed money. Richard's income is twenty times that of Jim's. Take a guess: who has more fun? The inward-mindset producer or one with the outward mindset?

Bill Bartman is the founder of CFS2 Bill Collection Company. While this is not a very sexy operation, Bartman created this company because of hard times in his own life. You know the drill. Collectors call you incessantly until they get you on the telephone, threatening to damage your credit unless you promise to pay a bill. Even though you won't be thrown into prison, as happened in the nineteenth century, the process is still embarrassing and extremely difficult to get through.

Bartman soon realized that people didn't pay their bills because they didn't have the money to pay them. An inward mindset would focus on the process of bill collection; calling, threatening, and browbeating. But Bartman took an outward-mindset approach. He helped people pay their bills by helping them make more money. At first his team gave debtors budgeting advice. But that did not seem to work well. Those with debts were so beaten down that they had lost any motivation to make their lives better. Then the employees of CFS2 began by writing résumés for clients. They started looking for job opportunities, helped the clients fill out applications, and scheduled job interviews. They ran mock interviews to help their clients prepare for the real thing. Talk about an outward mindset! Bartman's staff even called clients the morning of job interviews reminding them of when to show up.

Bartman incentivizes staff not only for the bills they collect, but for the services they provide to clients. The results have been outstanding. CFS2's rate of collection has been twice as high as that of any other firm in the industry. Bartman created a company that has become a partner by helping clients want to pay instead of avoiding the collector. This is an example of how an outward mindset was not only a good thing to do in itself, but created stellar financial results for the company.

The San Antonio Spurs NBA team have stayed dominant in a supremely competitive sport. They have succeeded in spite of aging key players, turnover of team members, and constant contract negotiations and sometimes disputes. But Coach Gregg Popovich calls his team "a dynamically adaptive outward-mindset organism." The word *organism* is apt because each individual member acts as part of a team with a single identity. There is no ego on the floor to prevent the most advantageous moves from succeeding. This is truly remarkable in basketball. Former LA Laker Kobe Bryant would berate his team members unless they gave the ball to him.

The 1999 Houston Rockets were called "the dream team." They had Hakeem Olajuwon, Scottie Pippen, and Charles Barkley, among many other stars. They were also the highest-paid players in the NBA at the time. But these Rockets had a losing season because the dream team couldn't play together. They were a team of individuals with inward mindsets instead of a team with an outward mindset trying to help others succeed. When the whole team succeeds, the game is won. As you've heard in countless television commercials, there is no "I" in "team."

Popovich said the secret of his success was to look for players who have "gotten over themselves." He developed an outward mindset, creating a culture that gave the Spurs a competitive advantage. His success was based on four factors.

1. Recruiting and building selflessness and teamwork. Popovich called this "relationship excellence."
2. Caring for staff and players as people.
3. Giving players and staff a voice.
4. Achieving task excellence, enabled by relationship excellence.

Popovich said that discipline in a team, although it is always important, is not enough. Relationships are what it's about. He said "You have to make players realize you care about them; in turn they have to care about and be interested in each other."

With an outward mindset, Popovich again demonstrated that when you help people get what they want, they help you get what you want. The players feel a heightened obligation to build their skills and consistently perform at their best. This reinforces the point that when players dedicate themselves to something bigger than themselves, they achieve far greater results than they could when they are only focused on themselves.

THE GROWTH MINDSET

One of the most famous mindset researchers is Stanford psychologist Carol Dweck. She was very curious about understanding how people cope with failure. She studied children, at first giving them difficult puzzles to solve. One ten-year-old boy pulled up his chair, rubbed his hands together, smacked his lips, and said, "I love a challenge." Another student condescendingly said, "I was hoping this would be a challenge." One student was willing to put in his best effort, while the other dismissed the puzzle as not being unworthy of his effort. One was willing to try; the other, not at all.

Dweck began to wonder whether human qualities were carved in stone or whether performance could be improved by working harder. This question of talent versus hard work has been troubling psychologists for decades. When I was a graduate student in the 1970s, we studied nature versus nurture. At the time the belief was that although your talents and abilities are set in concrete, and you can make only minor improvements. The common wisdom was that about 80 percent of who you are, including your abilities and your future success, is in your talent. About 20 percent of your potential is what you do with that talent. Dweck turned that concept upside down.

We even had ways to measure your potential. One was the IQ (intelligence quotient) test. Today most people think that your IQ is your unchanging ability to learn. Even modern literature describes IQ as a fixed quantity that cannot be increased. The creator of the concept of IQ was Alfred Binet, a French psychologist working in Paris in the early twentieth century, wanted to identify children who were not profiting from the Paris public school system. He wanted to find those kids who would perform better from new educational programs so as to get them back on track.

When I was a sophomore in high school, I was in a history class I disliked. I toughed it out for a month and then visited my high-school counselor, asking to change classes. She said all the classes were full except for one, a gifted-student program. She told me that I had already been tested and that my IQ was not high enough to get in. I told her how much I disliked the class, and she finally relented. She gave me a new IQ test with a time limit of three hours. Discouraged, I took the test and reluctantly went back to my boring class. The next day the counselor called me into her office, looking shocked. She said I scored in the 99th percentile. She had never seen someone able to raise his IQ before. But the main reason she was ecstatic was that in those days schools received more grant money for finding high-IQ students. The problem was that they rarely ever tested anybody twice.

IQ also creates a self-image that affects the way you lead your life. It can determine your goals, your career, and even the things you think you have the ability to accomplish. Can you imagine all the kids who have been told that their average IQ was not enough to get them into medical or engineering school?

THE FIXED MINDSET

When you have a concept of yourself as limited by the talent and ability you already have, you are indeed limited. Dweck defined this as a *fixed mindset*. Fixed-mindset people believe they can never become Einsteins or Beethovens. They reason that if they had those gifts, someone would have identified them when they were young. The reason this mindset is so limiting is that if your dream was to become a physicist, and you were told you didn't have any talent for it, you would fail. If you failed, you would be rejected. If you got rejected, you would feel like a loser, so why even try? So a fixed mindset creates a limit to what you think you can accomplish. That will cause you to decrease your expectations and will limit your goals and even your lifestyle.

It's interesting that both Charles Darwin and the great Russian writer Leo Tolstoy started as ordinary children. Nobody picked them to be super achievers. Even Ben Hogan, one of the greatest golfers of all time, was completely uncoordinated as a child. You may have heard that Fred Astaire once did an audition in which the director let him know he was unimpressed. Astaire kept a memo over his fireplace from the MGM testing director after his first screen test that read, "Can't act. Slightly bald. Can dance a little." Even the great Michael Jordan was cut from his high-school basketball team. Jordan once said, "I've failed over and over again in my life, and that is why I continue to succeed."

While IQ may measure the ability to learn at the moment the test is given, there's no test to measure what someone's intelligence will be ten years from now. Many psychologists used to think that people constantly overrate their talents and abilities. The opposite is true. Studies show that people are actually terrible at estimating their own abilities. In fact you are likely to greatly misestimate your performance and ability. People with fixed mindsets are most likely to underestimate their abilities.

One of the oddities about IQ is what it really measures. Binet wanted to give students better learning outcomes. But IQ does not measure how smart you will be later. People with the growth mindset are quick to realize that IQ measures a moment in time, but not the future. Those with fixed mindsets are stuck with the notion that their measured IQ is all they will ever be.

One of the tragedies of mindset is the expectation teachers have of their students. If a teacher believes that a student has a high IQ, they will interact with that student differently. If a teacher believes the student has a low IQ, the teacher will lower their expectations. This was true when I was transferred to the gifted-student class. The teachers were more challenging and engaging than in the classes for those with lower IQs. The gifted-student teachers all thought there were developing the next brain surgeons and rocket scientists instead of just getting their students out the door to graduate.

There are many stories about students with genius-level IQ's who failed miserably in school. Einstein dropped out of school at one point. Bill Gates, of Microsoft fame, dropped out of Harvard, as did Facebook founder Mark Zuckerberg.

The teacher behind the movie *Stand and Deliver* thought differently. Garfield High School was one of the worst schools in Los Angeles. But math teacher Jaime Escalante thought all of the students could achieve excellence. He thought each student could possess a growth mindset. He asked, not *can* I teach these students, but instead, *how* can I teach these students? His attitude focused on how to teach them best, not on whether they could learn. Not only did he teach them calculus, but he took them to the top among all math classes nationwide. In 1987, there were only three other schools in the country that had more students taking the advanced college placement calculus test. His students all earned college credits. Because there were so few minorities at this advanced math level, many teachers before Escalante believed it was not worth their trouble. They thought these types of students were unable to learn.

I hear frequently of people who were grateful for a particular teacher who believed in them—a teacher who took extra time and invested hard work in helping them learn. Think how your life would have changed if all of your teachers had taken this attitude. That's what makes great teachers so special. They are those who believe, not in what you are now, but in who you can be. They do not have fixed mindsets, but growth mindsets, preparing you for the future.

Dweck also identified those with a growth mindset as people who believe that, through effort and focus, they can achieve what they want. Those with a growth mindset believe when they try harder in class, they get better grades. If they are more careful in driving their cars, they will get into fewer accidents. If they study harder and take graduate classes, they will advance their careers. Growth-mindset people believe that they can work harder to improve their lives. Fixed-mindset people believe there's nothing they can do. Who they are is all they will have.

Howard Gardner's book *Extraordinary Minds: Portraits of Four Exceptional Individuals and an Examination of Our Own Extraordinariness* says that exceptional people have a special talent for discovering their own strengths and weaknesses. Growth-mindset people know what they do well and what they are more challenged at. But unlike fixed-mindset people, those with a growth mindset believe they can improve both strengths and weaknesses.

Michael Jordan seems like the epitome of someone who was

born with great talent and ability. He was destined for his greatness. Commercials said, "Be like Mike." He was a demigod in tennis shoes. Nobody would dare to say he wasn't special. But Jordan once said, "I'm a person like anyone else." He wasn't special. His great success came because he worked so hard at developing his abilities. He had never seemed inherently better than anyone else. As we've seen, in 1978, when he was fifteen, he was cut by high-school basketball team. At only five feet ten, he couldn't even dunk a basketball. The fifteen players who made the team probably had more innate ability. Jordan might not have used these words, but he got past a fixed mindset and continued to grow.

At six feet, I too was cut by my freshman basketball team. But unlike Jordan, I never played basketball again. Too bad at age fifteen, I didn't know about the growth mindset.

In a fixed-mindset world, failure proves the limits of your talents and abilities. In a growth-mindset world, failure is a speed bump, a setback to getting what you want. Getting a bad grade is a setback on your way to getting straight A's. Losing a tennis tournament is a speed bump in getting closer to winning the next one.

But there is one especially powerful difference between fixed and growth mindsets. It's *effort*. In a fixed-mindset world, achievement should not take much effort. In a growth-mindset world, effort is what makes you smart and talented. Sociologist Benjamin Barber once said that he didn't divide the world into successes and failures, but into learners and non-learners.

What makes you a non-learner? One thing is *learned helplessness*. Young children don't quit as they are learning to walk. They don't stop themselves from talking when they first babble. They just barge ahead. It's only when we become self-aware that we start to learn that effort is not worth it.

When my daughter Catherine was ten, I enrolled her in an after-school girls' softball team. She was not the best player on the team, or the worst. But she constantly complained how bad she was in comparison with other girls. She didn't think she had the talent to be a good player. I kept pointing out how good she was compared to the worst girls on the team. But that was a mistake. I only verified to Catherine that she didn't have the talent to be the best. So she gave up. And I let her.

Fixed-mindset people look at effort simply as a proof of their own talent. Growth-mindset people look at effort as a stepping-stone to the next level. One of the reasons a fixed-mindset person fails is pessimism. *I knew that was not going to work! I can't believe I wasted all that time! I could've been doing something else!*

One of my best tennis friends, Warren, played a mixed-doubles match with a weak player and lost badly. Warren, a stockbroker with a major firm, is always engaging and funny. But after his loss that day, he said, "That's two hours of my life I will never get back." Warren meant that as a joke. But it's a common thought among fixed-mindset people. They view setbacks as wastes of effort instead of as stepping-stones to success.

Here are some statements that can help determine whether you are a fixed- or growth-mindset person. Keep track of which ones you agree and disagree with.

1. Your IQ is set, and you can't do much to change it.
2. You can learn new skills, but you really can't change your level of talent.
3. No matter what your IQ or talent is, you can always change it as much as you want.
4. You can substantially change your IQ.

How did you answer these questions? A "yes" to questions 1 and 2 indicate a fixed mindset. A "yes" to questions 3 and 4 indicate a growth mindset. You can also be a mixture of fixed and growth mindsets, although most people lean toward one or the other.

Think about some of your friends with fixed mindsets. They are always trying to prove themselves and are avoiding making mistakes. Is this you? Have you ever been this way?

Think about someone with a growth mindset. They believe talent and ability can be cultivated. Think about how they confront setbacks and obstacles. They believe they can get past any obstacle. They look at setbacks as opportunities to stretch themselves. Is this you? How do you face obstacles? Do you fold, or do you look at them as challenges that will help you get past the next ones?

One problem with fixed-mindset people is that when they succeed, they may feel superior. They feel their abilities are better than anyone else's. This feeds into a narrative that is very self-limiting, because when they fail, their superiority is put at risk. They may start blaming and making excuses and quit.

John McEnroe may have fit this fixed-mindset theory. In his book *You Cannot Be Serious*, he writes that he didn't love to learn. He didn't thrive on challenges. By his own admission, he didn't fulfill his potential. But he did believe in his own enormous talent. Talent alone catapulted him to the position of number one in the tennis world for four years.

Like Ivan Lendl, another tennis great, McEnroe used sawdust to get a better grip on his racket during hot days. Sawdust absorbs more sweat than anything else during a match. But one day he blamed the sawdust for his poor performance. He went over to the sawdust can and knocked it over with his racket. Yelling at his agent, Gary, he said, "You call that sawdust? It's ground too fine. This looks like rat poison. Can't you get anything right?" Gary took off, and twenty minutes later came back with a fresh can of coarser sawdust. Gary had actually paid a union employee twenty dollars to grind up a two-by-four.

George Herbert Walker Bush once threw up on the Japanese prime minister during a state dinner. Coincidentally, John McEnroe did the same thing on a Japanese lady who was hosting him. The dignified lady bowed, apologized, and presented him the next day with a gift. But with the superiority of a fixed mindset, McEnroe said, "This is what it's like to be number one."

Jim Marshall, a former Minnesota Vikings defensive player, had one of the most embarrassing games of his life. Against the San Francisco 49ers, Marshall scooped up a fumble and ran for a touchdown as the crowd cheered. The problem was that he ran the wrong way. He scored for the opposing team. To make matters worse, it was on national television. It was the most devastating game of his life. But possessing a true growth mindset, he thought, "If you make a mistake, you gotta make it right." Then he realized he had a choice. He could sit in misery or he could do something about it. Getting himself together, he played the best football of his career during the second half. The Minnesota Vikings won that game.

We all love to hear these rags-to-riches, failure-to-success stories. But the traits that create these successes can also translate to our own lives. With a growth mindset, you can learn to succeed. With a fixed mindset, you are caught in your own failure.

Imagine yourself in front of a class answering questions from a teacher. You give the wrong answers. If you are in a fixed mindset, your self-esteem is on the line. Your prestige and your image are at risk. Would you be embarrassed? Would your self-confidence take a hit? With a growth mindset, answering questions n front of a class is different. You are not the teacher, you are the learner. You're not expected to know what the teacher knows. You're expected to make mistakes. That's why you're a student. As you are corrected, you note the mistakes to learn from so that you can achieve better performance in the future. Which one are you? The emotionally battered student or the learner who takes a lesson away that he can use?

THE DUAL MINDSET

You are probably thinking that you are not all growth and not all fixed mindset. I'm like you. When a business setback occurs, I start thinking about preparing for a slowdown. When I get booked for a speech in front of thousands, I start thinking they booked me because I'm one of the smartest and best speakers in America. Neither is correct. When my business has a setback, I need to realize that I can regain momentum by reengaging with people I've connected with in the last year. When I'm booked for a major speech, I need to realize that it's only because of hard work that they booked me, and that preparing for the speech will require equal effort.

Vince Lombardi once said, "Success is never forever, and failure is never fatal." He said, "The difference is the courage to try." This is a very hard lesson to learn: not feeling arrogant when everything goes well, and not feeling limited and depressed when things go south. A growth mindset means that you can work your way out of a setback. A fixed mindset means that if great things don't happen, it's because you're not good enough. Although you may be a mixture of both fixed and growth mindsets now, you can replace the fixed mindset with an attitude that fosters growth.

One example of a dual mindset is Bob Knight, the great Hoosier basketball coach. Knight could be unbelievably kind. He once passed up a lucrative opportunity to be a sportscaster because a former player had been involved in an accident. Knight stayed by the player's side throughout the recuperation. When he coached the U.S. Olympic team at the 1984 Los Angeles games, he insisted that the team honor coach Henry Iba, who, he believed, had never been given respect for his accomplishments. Knight had the players carry Coach Iba around the floor on their shoulders.

But Knight had another side, the fixed-mindset side. As author John Feinstein wrote in *A Season on the Brink: A Year with Bob Knight and the Indiana Hoosiers*, Knight was incapable of accepting or dealing with failure. Every defeat was personal. Everyone existed to validate his ability. Every loss was unacceptable. Instead of growing from a loss, it destroyed him. If he believed that if a player didn't play up to his potential, the player was not allowed to ride back with the team: he was no longer worthy of respect. Once, after his team reached the semifinals of a national tournament, Knight was asked by an interviewer what he liked best about the team. He said, "What I like best about the team is that I only have to watch them play one more game!" After years of seeing players berated, assistant coaches would caution them not to listen to Knight's deprecations. They would say, "Just ignore it, he doesn't really mean it."

Knight's explosions were legendary. He once famously threw a chair across the court. Once he pulled a player by his jersey off the court. One of the worst was when he grabbed a player by the neck. I have played both high-school and college sports. A football coach who called me stupid was devastating. A college tennis coach once said I could never win with my weak return. Comments like that would cause me to doubt whether tennis was the right sport for me. Bob Knight said it was to toughen his players up to prepare them for pressurized games.

At times this fixed-mindset, hard-liner coaching system worked. Knight had three championship teams. At other times it didn't. Over the years some of his players transferred to other schools. They cut classes and skipped tutorial sessions. Some, like Isaiah Thomas, elected to enter early into the pros. The problem was that while Knight had a growth mindset about his players, he had a fixed mindset about himself. He believed that his players could become great, but anything diminishing his own ability, such as a loss, was unacceptable.

This duality of fixed and growth mindsets probably describes a lot of us. In some ways we support our kids and believe they can do anything. But if they make mistakes, it's a reflection on us and our bad parenting. We believe that our employees or coworkers have enormous potential. But when they make mistakes, it's a reflection on our bad management, and we reprimand the person without thought of developing them for the future. This again is a fixed/growth mindset combination. The best way to change is to catch yourself in the process of limiting people rather than using every opportunity to help them grow.

How do you cope with your own setbacks? Do you get discouraged? Do you get paralyzed? Or do you look at setbacks with the confidence that you can recover with hard work? With a fixed mindset, setbacks are seen as an indication of a lack of ability. In one psychological study, those with a fixed mindset were more likely to say that if they did poorly on a test, even one in a course they liked a lot, they would study less in the future and consider cheating on the next test. Once a fixed-mindset person has a setback, they think it shines a spotlight on their limited ability. With a rowth mindset, students who do poorly commit to studying harder for the next test. You've heard before that when the going gets tough, the tough get going. But nobody's probably ever told you that this applies exclusively to those with a growth mindset.

In another psychological study, students who suffered setbacks lost interest and confidence. As the difficulty increased, their commitment and joy decreased. As I mentioned in an earlier chapter, with ten-year-olds who were given a puzzle, one student said, "I love a challenge," while another student said, "I'm not good at these." Who do you think performed better on the test?

What this all means is that fixed-mindset people prefer looking good over learning how to be better. They fear effort when it's not guaranteed. They abandon the most effective strategies of hard work when they need it most.

Years ago, I watched the movie *Moneyball*. It featured a losing Oakland A's baseball team run by ex-player Billy Beane (played by Brad Pitt). Beane, by his own admission, was a natural baseball player. But like many pro athletes, he had setbacks he couldn't recover from. He said he was coddled by everyone until he got to the pros. He believed that his ability, not hard work, would carry him to fame. Luckily, Beane recovered from a fixed mindset and moved to one of growth. He led his team to many seasons of nearly record-breaking wins on one of the lowest budgets in baseball.

The team had a statistics guru that had calculated each pitcher's probability of success with every batter. He also measured each batter's likelihood of getting on base by stealing. Some of them ended up having more bases and runs than the ones who were better hitters. This is one of the earliest examples of quant (quantification) theory in sports.

My favorite line in the movie was when Beane told the statistics nerd to fire a player. The nerd said, "How I do that?" Beane said, "How do you think you should fire him?" The nerd said, "I think I'll tell him how much we've appreciated his effort, how much we value him as a player and how sorry we are to have him leave the team." Billy Beane then rolled his eyes and said, "If you were going to get shot, would you like five in the chest or one in the head?" In the next scene the nerd simply said to the expendable player, "We traded you to Atlanta. Here's your airplane ticket. I wish you well." To which the player simply said, "OK" and left. I like this story so much is because we think the people we work with are so fragile they can't take bad news. But I've always believed that being direct is always better than dancing around the issue.

MINDSET AND POTENTIAL

Many pro athletic team scouts look for players with natural ability. They look for athletes who look and move like superstars. If they didn't look the part, they were overlooked. Ben Hogan, one of the greatest golfers of all time, didn't have the grace of Bobby Jones. Cassius Clay (later Muhammad Ali) didn't have the reach, chest expansion, heft, or fist size of a natural heavyweight boxer. In fact people gave him no chance in his epic 1964 title bout against Sonny Liston. Liston was three inches taller and had a reach that was four inches longer than Clay's. When the eighth bell rang, Clay came to his corner, about to quit the fight. But he had a secret weapon in his manager, Angelo Dundee. Angelo said, "Keep fighting, you're about to win the match." But Clay was done. He even started to undo his gloves. But Dundee encouraged him to go one more round. He said that Liston was tired, spent, and beaten. All Clay had to do was stand up and fight one more round. When the bell rang, Dundee took the chair out from under Clay. He gave Cassius a wedgie, pulling up his shorts up, and even gave him a knee in the back to make him step forward. As he did that, a towel came into the ring from the Liston side. They gave up. Cassius Clay won the fight.

Sonny Liston should have won that fight. He was physically better. He was stronger. He looked like a better boxer. But thanks to Clay's desire and Dundee's courage, Muhammed Ali became perhaps the best heavyweight fighter in world history.

UNLIKELY SUCCESS

Running back Darren Sproles is another good example. Playing half-back for the San Diego Chargers, he set rushing records. When he played for the New Orleans Saints, he was even better. But when I tell you he is only five feet eight, you should be shocked. You would think that all a defensive linebacker had to do was stick his arm out and Sproles would be knocked down. But what Sproles possesses more than much bigger players is desire, work ethic, and speed. His agility and his ability to dart through offensive holes have made him one of the best running backs in the league.

In short, the view you have of yourself dramatically impacts how you lead your life. Your mindset can determine whether you become the person you want to be and accomplish the things that you aspire to.

3

How to Build a Results-Focused Mindset

When I was in graduate school, one intense area of study was cognitive psychology. A metaphor given to help us learn this field better was how computer code is written. Each code is created with a result in mind. The final computer program is the creation of thousands of lines of code, which make a computer work. Mindset works the same. Your mindset is comprised of millions of lines of code you have created. The behavior your mindset produces in turn creates the results you experience in your life.

At this point we've spoken about what a mindset is and have even discussed why it's critical to develop an outward mindset instead of an inward one. We've talked about the notion that mindset creates behavior, and behaviors in turn create habits. We've also talked about how your beliefs and values influence your mindset and attitude. But you're probably reading this book because you want to improve your results by changing to a more constructive, outward, growth-focused mindset. In other words, you want to change.

I have to admit that I've really never believed that people can change. During seminars, I usually spend at least fifteen to twenty minutes talking about the fact that people don't change. Of the Americans married this year, 62 percent will be divorced in ten years. How about second marriages? Do you think the percentage is higher or lower? Yes, it's much higher. The divorce rate for second marriages within ten years is 78 percent. (During seminars I jokingly say, "The reason it's so high is because you took yourself with you to the second marriage!") Are you wondering about third marriages? This time around, divorce rates decrease to 36 percent within ten years. It's probably because people realize they've messed up two marriages, so they'll work hard to avoid failing with the third.

Prison recidivism is 83 percent within five years after getting out of jail. I don't think it's because the food is so good and the sports are so much fun that convicts can't wait to get back. I think it's because people have a very difficult time changing. I could go on for hours about this, but suffice it to say that your personality, values, ethics, and even how you think were substantially developed by the time you hit the age of seven. The great developmental psychologist Jean Piaget once said that personality is created and completed between two and seven years old.

But don't be discouraged. While I believe that people have an enormously difficult time changing their mindsets, they *can* learn. And the harder you work on applying what you learn, the more you'll be able to develop a better mindset.

The mindset that combines both the outward and growth-oriented aspects and will serve you best is the Results-Focused Mindset. Becoming outwardly minded and knowing how your decisions will affect others is important. You can't maintain a healthy, productive mindset without considering others. At the same time a growth-focused mindset will maintain your motivation and enable you to believe that anything is possible as long as you work hard enough. Being growth-focused will help you create optimism and will remind you that your genes and talent account for a very small part of your success.

A combination of both growth and outward mindsets is the Results-Focused Mindset. This is one that will allow you to keep an end result in mind. It will also help you stay positive when setbacks occur, maintaining your motivation in spite of discouragement. The Results-Focused Mindset doesn't just help you learn from mistakes, as the growth mindset by itself does, it helps you apply those lessons toward a goal.

Years ago, I spoke at a road show in the financial services industry. The speech was in Manchester, New Hampshire. I had a partnership with the company putting on the seminar and asked the wholesaler if one of my local clients could attend. But the guest was a competitor and inappropriately tried to recruit the attendee he sat next to. It wasn't until the next month at another seminar in Boston that I heard about the infraction. The wholesaler accused me of setting my guest up to steal her business. I said it was an outrageous accusation, since I was doing more than fifty seminars a year for this company. What would I jeopardize that relationship? But she didn't back down, and I saw only danger in protesting my innocence. I asked what I could do to rebuild the trust. We decided that I would waive my speaking fee for that one speech in Boston. I asked if that could be the end of the incident. She agreed.

A month later, another wholesaler from the same company called me from Chicago and canceled my three speeches with him. The Boston wholesaler had, on a nationwide company conference call, accused me of sabotaging her business. This was the wholesaler I had waived my speaking fee for, the same wholesaler who said the issue was resolved after I spoke at her meeting for free.

The deceit was obvious. The infraction was deleterious. With a fixed mindset, only blame would make me feel better. With a growth mindset, I would just work harder. But with a Results-Focused Mindset, the setback just spurred me to be more creative in bypassing this company, which had given me so much business, and took me in a new direction to hit my goals that year. Since then I have learned never to depend on one company or one industry for so much business. I have also learned to be more careful when allowing guests to attend, and I am more sensitive to any conflicts a guest may bring.

All of us have our stories of being wronged or slighted. But with a Results-Focused Mindset, we can take those lessons and achieve our goals more effectively. All of us can learn to be more productive. How do you succeed? By gaining wisdom. How do you gain wisdom? By learning from your mistakes. How do you learn from your mistakes? By making them.

RECASTING YOUR MINDSET

One technique you can use to develop a Results-Focused Mindset is called *recasting*. As I've written in my books *Willpower: The Secrets of Self Discipline* and *Mastering Self-Confidence with NLP*, there are very specific things you can do today to create a more effective mindset.

Recasting works much like a frame around a picture. A poor frame can make any painting look worse, just as a beautiful frame can make even a mediocre painting look substantially better. In some cases, the frame can look better than the picture itself. Recasting is built on the concept that there are no good or bad events in your life; there's only your perception.

One of my favorite stories about one's perception of results is from the movie *Charlie Wilson's War*. The story is about how jaded congressman Charlie Wilson (played by Tom Hanks) was able to help the Afghan Mujahedeen warriors defeat the Soviets in the 1980s, during the Reagan administration. (This also led to the start of the Al-Qaeda terrorist movement, but that is another story.)

A CIA officer, played by the late Philip Seymour Hoffman, cautions Wilson not to be too sure they have done something glorious. To make the point, he tells the story of a Zen master who observes the people of his village celebrating a young boy's new horse as a wonderful gift. "We'll see," the Zen master says. When the boy falls off the horse and breaks a leg, everyone says the horse is a curse. "We'll see," says the master. Then war breaks out, the boy cannot be conscripted because of his injury, and everyone now says the horse was a fortunate gift. "We'll see," the master says again. The moral of our story is that you can recast your perception of outcomes. You can change your mindset. You can change your results.

Recasting is not exactly visualization. It is more a rethinking or restructuring of how you think about a concept or idea. For example, if you decide to go into work at 7 a.m., your first inclination might be to think, "If I go in that early, I will feel tired." To recast that idea, you might think, "If I go into work at 7 a.m., I will be able to get an extra two hours of work done without interruption. This in turn will help me to achieve my goals more effectively."

I once developed a friendship with an airline pilot. His emotional picture frame was his flying career. He connected everything to flying or something related to it. If he saw a news report about Paris, he'd talk about a recent trip there. If we discussed food, he'd bring up airline cuisine.

Most people don't structure their thoughts to that extent, but we all see life in a way that either limits or empowers us. While my friend saw his experiences through the filter of aviation, it certainly served his objective of being a successful pilot. The way he framed the world made even the drudgery of his work enjoyable, because he saw the entire world as if it were related to flying.

You can use recasting to develop a Results-Focused Mindset. The key to recasting is to associate positive experiences with your goals and objectives and to disregard the obstacles, or at least to see them as opportunities to learn and cope. If you can do this, you'll have much more control over your life.

CONTEXT AND CONTENT RECASTING

Two types of recasting that will change your attitude away from the negative to the positive aspects of a new mindset are *context* and *content recasting*.

Context Recasting

Context recasting refers to your ability to take a negative situation and make it positive in another context. For example, say your flight is delayed four hours because of weather. You could become irritated, as most passengers would be, or you could get four hours of work done without interruption. With a fixed mindset, you would curse the airline. With a Results-Focused Mindset, you would relish the chance to use the extra time constructively.

I was recently stuck in the Newark airport, which has the highest number of delays in America. Passengers were irate when a United Airlines flight was canceled. Instead of becoming angry, I picked out a chair next to a power plug and started to work on this book. I was actually pretty happy that I had time to get some work done. (A recent BizTravel news report showed that only 15 percent of travelers take advantage of travel as an opportunity to work or get things done. Most sleep or simply stare into space.)

I have written four books while flying on airplanes. This could not have been accomplished if all my flights had been on time, nor could it have been accomplished if I hadn't taken advantage of the extra time that became available to me. Even so, recasting is more than making lemons into lemonade. It is thinking of your experiences as challenges and turning them into benefits.

At one time the 3M Corporation had trouble with the durability of one of its adhesives. The company's goal was to sell more of it, but the defect made for dwindling sales. Although the adhesive was not effective at bonding materials permanently, it did bond them temporarily. One researcher used recasting and put just a little bit of the adhesive on the back of a piece of paper to make it stick to nearly any surface. Was there an application this adhesive could be used for? You guessed it—Post-it Notes were born.

Here is another example of a context recast:

There once was a farmer who owned an old mule. The mule fell into the farmer's well. The farmer heard the mule braying, but after assessing the situation, he decided that neither the mule nor the well was worth the trouble of saving. Instead he called his neighbors together and told them what had happened and enlisted them to help haul dirt to bury the old mule in the well and put him out of his misery.

Initially, the old mule was hysterical. But as the farmer and his neighbors continued shoveling and the dirt hit his back, a thought struck him. It suddenly dawned on him that every time a shovel load of dirt landed on his back, he would shake it off and step up. This he did, over and over again. Shake it off and step up . . . Shake it off and step up . . . Shake it off and step up . . .

No matter how distressing the situation seemed, the old mule fought panic and just kept right on shaking it off and stepping up.

It wasn't long before the old mule, battered and exhausted, stepped triumphantly over the wall of that well. What seemed that it would bury him had actually blessed him, all because of the manner in which he handled his adversity.

Content Recasting

The second type of recasting, content recasting, is the mental act of changing what an event means to you. For example, a Christian looks at death not as the end of life but as a new beginning in the kingdom of heaven.

For a more down-to-earth example, take an entrepreneur who recently went bankrupt selling commodities in Chicago. He now has a successful business that consists of several busy hot-dog shops. He describes his first business failure as getting an intense education in running a business.

Think of a project you've been putting off. Maybe it's something like repairing a piece of furniture. You can choose to see the job as taking away from the time you'd otherwise spend watching sports on TV, or you can choose to see yourself working on the repair, listening to the game on the radio, and enjoying the experience more than you would had you actually been watching TV.

This technique works. You simply have to change the negative image of working on the furniture to one where you're having fun. You can even recast an image to include your whole family helping and telling jokes. If you do this, your attitude toward the dreaded experience *will* change.

If this technique seems unbelievably simplistic, think of the last time you did the gardening or another household chore you'd been putting off. Didn't you avoid it for a long time, only to feel after you'd done it that the experience wasn't so bad after all?

My friend, sports commentator Terry Bradshaw, tried his hand as a motivational speaker. He took what he learned from the field and the speaking stage to the TV sports desk and recast his attitude and image in a way that empowered him to achieve his goals. He knew he wasn't as articulate as basketball great John Wooden, nor did he have the speaking flair of my client, Minnesota NFL Hall of Fame quarterback Fran Tarkenton, or even the attention to detail of Washington Redskins quarterback Joe Thiesman, but he did have a huge amount of enthusiasm. So he worked on developing a flair for enthusiastic delivery in a way that every audience would find contagious.

The difference between recasting and just being positive is the permanence with which the new thought lasts. If you replace old negative memories with new positive perspectives, you will be able to keep past events from limiting your future success. This in turn will help you change your mindset.

RECASTING EMOTIONS, BEHAVIORS, AND MEMORIES

It is even possible to recast emotions, behaviors, and memories. This technique is based on understanding neurolinguistic programming (NLP), first developed by researchers John Grinder and Richard Bandler. The theory goes that your unconscious controls how you experience and perceive both past memories and current events. It consequently controls all sorts of habitual behaviors, which frees you to think about more important and urgent things. For instance, you don't consciously think about braking your car when you come to a stop sign, but you brake nonetheless. That you unconsciously do so frees you to think consciously about the scenery, people, or conversations around you.

However, such unconscious habits may not always be good for you. In some cases, such as when you try to diet, your mindset may turn inward and may become negative. A couple of years ago, I spoke to a woman who had enormous trouble losing weight. She had tried every diet she could think of, and still nothing worked. After several conversations, I learned she had been raped as a teenager. She still struggled with that memory, as well as with the low self-esteem she'd had ever since. She was attractive, but her poor self-image was hard to alter after twenty-five years. Because of this low self-esteem, she found it impossible to lose weight. The extra weight simply confirmed her poor self-image. Being thin violated how she saw herself, so she was unable to lose the weight.

Like this woman, we need to find ways to influence our unconscious to get it to support our goals. To do this, we first need to know how you process information.

NLP holds that people basically perceive the world in one of three different ways: in pictures, sounds, or feelings.

Picture people make sense of the world by constructing or recalling images in their minds. If they can't make a mental picture of what you're saying, they may have trouble getting a clear understanding of your ideas.

Sound people make decisions largely on the basis of what they hear. They make sense of what they hear based on how things sound. They often talk to themselves in order to understand a message.

Feeling people tend to react viscerally. They get a gut emotion while talking to you. They may feel hot or cold about you or an idea after just a few minutes of interaction. Many people call this *intuition*.

If you knew what system you use to perceive the world, could you change your mindset? You bet. The following approach focuses on your unconscious thought mode to help you recast your emotions, behaviors, and memories so they are more supportive of a Results-Focused Mindset.

Here is the four-step approach to recasting emotions, behaviors, and memories. If you use these steps, you will improve your mindset.

1. Identify the pattern of behavior or thought you would like to change. For example, many athletes think in visual terms. Many of my tennis buddies tell me they pick a place on the court to serve to. Then they visualize the spot in their minds as they hit the ball.

If you want to hit a serve differently, you might imagine the spin the ball after it leaves the racquet instead of focusing on the mechanics of holding the racquet. One way to use visualization is for a slice serve in tennis (that is, a hit with sidespin). You might imagine the racket glancing off the side of the ball. You could picture the tennis ball being peeled like an orange by your racquet. You might also imagine the ball jumping straight up as it lands on the other side of the court. This would give you a very powerful mental image in tennis. But it is also an example of how to use visualization in any other task you want to accomplish.

In 1977, I was struggling while playing a professional tournament in Linz, Austria. I had only competed on clay courts for a few months, and still had trouble moving on this unstable surface. My serves didn't have the same kick and speed as on the hard courts I was used to. The clay surface caught the ball and slowed it down. The harder I tried to hit the ball, the more mistakes I made. I lost five games in a row and became desperate.

I had just finished a book by Tim Gallwey entitled *The Inner Game of Tennis*. Gallwey was the Zen master of tennis. His teaching method—really NLP before there was NLP—was to focus, not on how you hit the ball, but on the result. This technique was totally different from any teaching method up to that time. I was desperate and ready for anything. After all, if I kept making the same mistakes, I would lose the match.

I picked out a pebble on the clay surface where I wanted my serve to land, and just let it rip. My ball landed within inches of the target and aced the German national champion, who was my opponent that day. My next serve was a slice and kicked so high that it caught my opponent totally off guard.

The result: my service game immediately improved, and I won the match. This happened because I concentrated more on the result and the goal than on the method to reach them. Methods are always important, but sometimes we get so stuck in technique and process that we paralyze ourselves.

2. Use signals from your unconscious to determine the background reason for your unwanted behavior and to help change a habit pattern. (Most of our habitual behaviors and thoughts are unconscious anyway.) The way to go about this is to make your mind go blank and then pose a question to which you are looking for a "yes" or "no" answer. Separate the difference between the background reason for the behavior and the behavior itself. Again, do this by using unconscious signals that can be answered with "yes" and "no" questions.

Identify a new, desirable behavior that is more in line with your goals. Use your unconscious to help, using "yes" and "no" questions as a guideline.

Determine whether the new behavior fits in with who you are without inner conflict. Again, use "yes" and "no" questions as guidelines. For example, say the woman in our previous example continued to try to lose weight, but her unconscious didn't support this goal. Using step one, she would identify her eating habits as the behavior she wanted to change. Being thinner would be the goal to which she was consciously committed.

The next step in this process would be to get a signal from her unconscious about this goal. Again, the key to tapping into your unconscious is to think of questions with "yes" or "no" answers. Then clear your mind and pose these questions to your unconscious. The answers, negative or positive, won't come in words. They will be more of an image or feeling, or even what you hear yourself thinking.

This is because some of the most common signals our unconscious sends us are based on our dominant thought mode. If your most powerful mode is using pictures, for example, be passively aware of signals like images in your mind. Are those images dark, light, or small? The way your unconscious may signal you is by changing those images. It may make an image smaller, signaling "no," or brighter, signaling "yes." Some people will even see a flashing "yes" in the mental picture as a response to a question.

If you want to lose weight, can you picture yourself as thin? Is the image pleasing? Is the image of a thin body bright and big, or dim and small? If it's dim and small, your unconscious may not be supportive of your weight-loss program.

If your dominant mode is auditory, be aware of noises like ringing or other sounds that become louder or quieter when there is opposition. Can you hear people telling you how thin you look? Or do you hear ridicule because you're too thin? If your most powerful mode is feeling, watch for physical sensations. You might become aware that your fingers are tingling, or your legs might get warmer in response to the questions you ask. You also might get a feeling in your gut. Do you feel warmly excited about being thin, or do you feel dread as you contemplate the work it will take to lose weight? All of these signals are common, but you may feel others as well. Just remain aware of any signals your unconscious wants to use as you ask for "yes" or "no" answers to questions.

You might be thinking how silly it is to pay attention to your dominant thought mode as you evaluate your goals. But you do this all the time. You get a feeling before you buy something. You hear a voice in your head that something may not be right. You visualize problems or get excited about future opportunities. With the technique I'm describing, we are just using NLP to tap into the processes you are already using.

Tapping into your unconscious is essential to determining the background reason for any unwanted behavior. Ask your questions, and then be alert for answers that come from the dominant mode your body is reacting to. The woman who wanted to lose weight discovered there was a secondary gain to being overweight—diminished attention from men. By asking herself questions, she determined that her unconscious resisted losing weight, because being heavy saved her from the pressure of dating.

To get your unconscious to stop protecting you through this secondary behavior, you need to acknowledge what it has been doing. Then you need to ask if there are other ways to protect yourself from the perceived threat besides the undesired behavior. Again, use a series of "yes" and "no" questions to learn what these alternatives might be.

In the case of the overweight woman, she might have asked her unconscious if she could protect herself from the pressures of dating by deciding not to go out with anyone for a certain period of time. Another question she could have asked was whether dating was really all that threatening. You see how it goes. Asking these questions occurs in a sort of stream of consciousness, in which one question leads to another.

Keep in mind, though, from time to time all of us see secondary gains in not changing our mindset. My tardiness in practicing the trumpet at age twelve grew out of my dislike of the instrument. I was consequently late to lessons and procrastinated practicing, but I was never late to baseball or tennis practice.

Likewise, procrastination in going back to college may lie in an unconscious desire not to leave your job as a waitress or bartender. Maybe you really like this job, even though you don't make enough money. The truth is, you don't procrastinate doing the things you love. If you think you want the goal, but still procrastinate, you need to get your unconscious involved to find out why.

I once read a report about a pro golfer who, ten years earlier, had been ranked in the top twenty in the world. He hadn't won a tournament in these ten intervening years and thought he had the "yips," a tendency to hit the ball with a jerk instead of a smooth controlled swing. It's sort of like trying to be extra careful around expensive china and then nervously breaking it all.

The interviewer asked some probing questions about the pro's family, and discovered that his spouse wasn't especially supportive. She wanted him to take a job as a local country-club pro. He felt guilty about all the travel time away from his family, and had trouble committing to his demanding goal enough to get back into the top twenty.

3. Create a new behavior in line with your goals. Again, let's use the example of the woman who wanted to lose weight. She found,

through her unconscious, that she had a secondary gain from doing just the opposite (it saved her from the pressure of dating). A solution for her was to change her goal of how much weight she would lose—say ten pounds instead of twenty-five. This way her behavior still changed, her goals were still met, and her unconscious had time to adjust. Thus she would be more readily able to support a further weight loss in the future if she so desired.

4. Make sure the new behavior is in line with your unconscious goals. The woman who wanted to lose weight tried to get a sense of her new self-confidence in the context of, "Is this really what I want, consciously and unconsciously?" As she checked her unconscious by using "yes" and "no" questions, she also made a commitment to uncover new ways and techniques to take the weight off and keep it off. She then used the unconscious signals she had previously accessed to try to get her unconscious to embrace her goal of losing weight. Once she had done all these things, she was ready to work toward achieving her objective, albeit a little at a time.

When you use the techniques of visualization and recasting, self-confidence can be like Aladdin's lamp—it can grant you just about anything you wish for. All you have to do is know how to rub the lamp. As the old saying goes, beware what you wish for. You may get it!

ASSIGNMENTS

- Look at a person close to you and then look away. Describe to yourself verbally or in writing what that person looks like, without looking back. Be as detailed as possible. Then look again and compare your list with how that person actually looks. As you practice this activity, you will get better at visualization.

- Think back on a pleasurable experience. See it in your mind. Notice the vividness of the images. Now turn up the intensity of the color, proximity, and brightness. Do you feel even happier and more excited?

  Then imagine a bad experience, say of getting depressed because of a setback, and see if you can turn down the vividness to avoid a fixed-mindset response. Make your picture of this experience dimmer. See it off in the distance, black and white, dull and fuzzy. See if you can do this enough to reduce the bad feelings you attach to this event. Does the different image help you to think of the event merely as a setback that you can learn from?

- Think of a goal you would like to work toward and, as applicable, use content and context recasting as we described earlier to help reshape your mindset toward achieving this goal. With content recasting, you can change what a goal means to you. Using context recasting, you can enhance the positive aspects of the goal or diminish the negative.

- Use the four-step technique to recast emotions, behaviors, and memories and commit yourself to the goal you identified in the previous activity.

4

Framing Your Results-Focused Mindset

During a momentous battle, a Japanese general decided to attack, even though his army was greatly outnumbered. He was confident they would win, but his men were filled with doubt. On the way to the battle, the army stopped at a religious shrine. After praying with his men, the general took out a coin and said, "I shall now toss this coin. If it is heads, we shall win. If it is tails, we shall lose. Destiny will now reveal itself."

He threw the coin into the air, and all watched intently as it landed. It was heads. The soldiers were so overjoyed and filled with confidence that they vigorously attacked the enemy and were victorious.

After the battle, a lieutenant remarked to the general, "No one can change destiny."

"Quite right," the general replied as he showed the lieutenant the coin, which had heads on both sides.

A few years ago, a New Jersey family was returning home from out of state after visiting relatives. When they approached the state line, they were shocked by what they saw. On the turnpike was a sign that read, "The State of New Jersey is closed." To make matters worse, a policeman stood next to the sign, apparently enforcing the closure. As the mom and dad exited the car, they stared for a long time at the sign, wondering when the state would reopen. When they finally asked the trooper when they could enter, Candid Camera producer Allen Funt walked out, explaining that they were on TV.

Would you fight a difficult battle with the odds stacked against you? You would if you believed you would win. Would you fall for something as silly as your state being closed? The answer is the same: you would if you believed, no matter how ridiculous it might seem upon reflection. As Julius Caesar said over two thousand years ago, "Men willingly believe what they wish."

Unfortunately, some of us, believe when we shouldn't, like the parrot in this short joke.

Once upon a time, a magician was working on a cruise ship in the Caribbean. The audience was different each week, so the magician allowed himself to do the same tricks over and over again.

There was only one problem: the captain's parrot saw the shows every week and began to understand what the magician did in every trick. Once he understood that, he started shouting in the middle of the show, "Look, it's not the same hat!" "Look, he's hiding the flowers under the table!" "Hey, why are all the cards the ace of spades?"

The magician was furious, but was unable to do anything about the parrot; it belonged to the captain, after all. One day the ship had an accident and sank. The magician found himself on a piece of wood in the middle of the ocean with the parrot by his side. They stared at each other with hate, but neither uttered a word. This went on for several days. After a week the parrot finally said, "OK, I give up. What'd you do with the boat?"

As this story makes clear, beliefs have nothing to do with reality. Instead, beliefs are the foundation of the saying, "Whether you think you can or you think you can't, you're right."

This is a good thing. It means we can change or alter our beliefs at any time to support the self-confidence required to meet our goals.

A short time ago, I was touring the island nation of Singapore during the religious festival of Thaipusam. This is a Hindu celebration in which the faithful give thanks and offer atonement for spiritual transgressions. During the ceremony I watched believers from virtually every walk of life piercing their skin by putting long, slender rods in their mouths and then through their cheeks. The surprising fact was that not one of the hundreds who pierced themselves bled. This is just one example of the force that belief can have in our lives, a force that apparently even has control over bodily functions such as bleeding when wounded.

Think of what the rest of us could accomplish if we could harness our beliefs to this extent. Could you improve your mindset? If you had this kind of control, changing your mindset to achieve your goals would be a snap. It's the kind of belief a young boy on a Little League baseball team had. When asked by a latecomer to the game what the score was, the boy replied with a smile, "We're behind fourteen to nothing." "Really," the latecomer said. "I have to say you don't look very discouraged." "Discouraged?" the boy asked with a puzzled look on his face. "Why should we be discouraged? We haven't been up to bat yet."

Earlier I discussed how visualizing success can affect our behavior. After all, images power our beliefs as well as the doubt that shakes them. Doubt exists when there's insufficient faith in a belief, but belief exists when there's a commitment to accepting something that may not always be provable.

Your beliefs influence your mindset. But it's important to realize that doubt too is a kind of belief. To demonstrate this point, think of one of your very strong beliefs. This belief might be religious, ethical, or even related to the way you do business. Try to get a visual image of that belief and what it's done for you in the past. You might recall something that you prayed for that came to pass, or a situation in which ethics paid off. Perhaps it's your strong belief in the concept of freedom, symbolized by the Statue of Liberty, or your belief that good things come to those who wait. This could be symbolized by the image of, say, your grandmother, who struggled through the accidental death of the abusive man she'd married at nineteen, but then met and married the loving, supportive man who became your grandfather.

Now try to picture something you doubt—something that may or may not be true. You might think of extraterrestrial beings and represent them in your mind with a picture of a flying saucer. Or you might think of your secret desire to be the head of your department at work, which may seem very improbable right now. You could envision a large, sunny office with a cherry-wood desk.

Now notice the visual differences in the pictures that represent your belief and your doubt. You probably see the belief picture as big, detailed, bright, and colorful, while the picture of what you doubt is probably much smaller, fuzzier, maybe only in black and white.

If you pay attention to your emotional and physical processes, you'll probably notice that when you visualize an important belief, you breathe slowly and deeply. Your hands may get warmer as the blood flow increases in your body. When you experience doubt, you become stressed. Your breathing will become shallower and your hands will grow cold and clammy.

This is one reason why people who believe in something are so much more courageous than those in doubt. Strong beliefs can make us brave to the point that we are even willing to give our lives. How else can the willingness of Islamic extremists to offer themselves as suicide bombers be explained? Very few, on the other hand, feel passionate about things they doubt. I haven't met many passionate atheists, have you? I have met a few people who don't believe in God, but not many who would die for that belief.

The great thing about belief is that it's always a choice. Your mindset can be changed if you can change your beliefs that don't support it. If your goal is to succeed at running a business, yet you have a fixed mindset and find yourself quitting, you can change your belief that it isn't worth the effort. Or enhance the belief that you can achieve any goal if you work hard and stick with it long enough.

We can choose beliefs that limit us, or beliefs that create power in our lives. Let's say you want to stop smoking, but you've tried and been unsuccessful. Did you believe from the start that you could accomplish your goal? Did you expect to be successful?

Think of the power you'd have, when taking on the goal of quitting smoking or losing weight or completing a report, if you believed from the start that you could do it. You could change your mindset and become less stressed. All along you'd approach the goal from a position of success instead of doubt. That belief in your own ability would serve to build the mindset you want.

Give it some thought. Then use the two following exercises to try to change the way you approach your goal, whatever it might be.

List an outcome you'd like to achieve, and write all the things you know about yourself that will help turn this outcome into reality. (I'll say more about the difference between goals and outcomes in chapter 6.) As you develop your list, think about whether you have the determination and drive to complete the task. Remind yourself of the positive traits and the high work ethic that you possess and which will support your success in achieving the goal. Chances are, you already have the talent and ability to accomplish what you want. All you need is to strengthen your internal belief, then forget about the things that might hold you back. Review this list every time you doubt your ability to finish a task. This will help shore up your belief in your ability to reach any goal you set.

I play tennis during the week with a group of younger guys who are better than I am, or at least not as injured as I am. My goal during every match is to play well. Often I remember only too well the bad days, when I missed easy shots. But when I focus on the matches in which I have played well, my mindset dramatically improves from one of "I hope I don't play crappy again" to "I am not judging my strokes, I am just going to have fun and play the best I can."

One of the court directors at Palisades Tennis Club in Newport Beach, California, heard a player talk about his bad match. Patty said, "Are you collecting a paycheck out there? Just play your match and stop complaining!" I loved that comment. We get so wrapped up in ourselves that we forget why we are there. Just enjoy the moment.

Review the positive traits you identified above and imagine yourself applying them to your outcome. Make a picture of each. Images about these supportive actions should be large, bright, and vivid. Any negative thought should be dim, black, and small. This will reduce the effect of doubt.

It's easier to use beliefs if you understand where they come from. Beliefs don't develop because someone hit you on the head one day while declaring what you can and can't believe. Rather, beliefs, and therefore your mindset, develop from four very tangible sources: our surroundings; what we discover intellectually; our experiences; and our hopes and expectations.

Surroundings   You know that childhood has a great effect on your success later in life. As discussed in an earlier section, if you grew up in a lower middle-class neighborhood, it might be hard for you to achieve great wealth in your life. This is due to a mindset that is telling you that just paying the bills is a struggle. But if your name were DuPont, Rockefeller, or Rothschild, your expectations and beliefs would be quite different. You would be comfortable around money because your parents always were. And they would have taught you how to manage it.

Usually, but not necessarily. Think about the Vanderbilts. According to one account, in 1800 Cornelius Vanderbilt borrowed $100 from his father to buy a ferry in New York. Later he built a shipping line and made his real money in railroads. At its zenith the family was worth $300 billion in today's dollars. (Last I checked, Jeff Bezos was the richest man in the world with only $82.5 billion.) But only three generations later, the Vanderbilt heirs were not worth even $1 million each. Some say they squandered the money. I think it's more than that. I think they didn't teach their heirs the lessons of how to manage it. By spending just 4 percent of the fortune every year, they could have maintained and even grown their wealth. It's all about mindset. The heirs had a fixed mindset instead of a growth mindset. They saw themselves as limited instead of able to grow what they had.

Ask yourself; are the outcomes you desire now consistent with the surroundings you experienced when you grew up? If they're not, can you cope with the differences in lifestyle these outcomes might bring? If you're a salesperson trying to make more money, do you believe you can cope with the changes that greater wealth will bring? Do you believe you really want money and greater wealth?

You're probably answering an enthusiastic "Yes!" but be careful: if you don't really believe you can or should make a higher income, you'll unconsciously sabotage your mindset in your attempt to do so.

To see if your beliefs are compatible with your goal of making more money, employ a technique called *future belief check*. In your mind, see a visual representation of a specific outcome you desire. Now see an image of yourself with that outcome to determine whether or not you think you deserve it. How vivid can you make that picture? Is it bright? Is it large? Is it colorful? If it isn't, this outcome may not be consistent with your beliefs. You can't change your mindset without first changing your beliefs. You need either to change the outcome or to change your belief.

Intellect   The second source of beliefs is your intellect. Here's how to use your intellect to check your beliefs. Take the same outcome you used in the last example. See the picture in your mind, and check to see if you believe you're intelligent enough to achieve that outcome. If your outcome is to complete college, do you believe you have enough of a work ethic to get good grades? It isn't about your IQ. It's about whether you will put in the effort. Your friends may know that you will, but do *you* know it? Imagine wearing a graduation gown, or carrying an armload of books, and check for the vividness, brightness, and size of the image. When we get discouraged and quit, we lose the image of the goal and outcome.

Experiences   The third source of beliefs is experiences. If you've been successful achieving things in the past, you'll likely be successful in the future. But if you've quit in the past, you may find it difficult to change your mindset to overcome obstacles in the future. However, it's not impossible. Let's try the belief check again. Imagine your outcome once more, and next to it envision a past failure. Then try to see the outcome as completed, shored up by your experience of the past. Is that picture vivid, large, and well defined? Will your past experience give you the self-confidence you need to succeed in the future to achieve this specific outcome? The picture and its characteristics will give you a good idea of the answer.

I try to complete my goals in everything I do. I have a belief and mindset that if I quit in the small things, I will quit in the big ones as well. When I am on the elliptical for a workout and plan a thirty-minute workout, pain starts at about the twenty-minute mark. I think about stopping, thinking that I should get to the office earlier. But then I try to see an image of what it's like to lose ten pounds and take pressure off of the arthritic disks in my back.

Hopes and Expectations   The fourth source of beliefs is our hopes and expectations of the future. Unless we hope very strongly for something, this is one of the hardest ways to develop strong beliefs. That's because there are so few tangible things other than faith on which to base future expectations. Even so, most of us probably have a belief right now that when we go to work tomorrow, we'll have a good day. Being able to develop a belief in future success is the lifeblood of any goal, especially for commissioned businesses like sales.

Little Jamie Scott is a good example of hopes and expectations. Jamie was trying out for a part in a school play and had his heart set on being in it, but his mother feared he would not be chosen.

After school on the day the parts were awarded, Jamie rushed up to his mom, his eyes shining with pride and excitement. "Guess what, Mom!" he shouted. "I've been chosen to clap and cheer!"

Often a person's beliefs come from a combination of these four factors. A friend of mine is a classic example of someone whose beliefs come from her intellect and experiences rather than her surroundings, hopes, or expectations. Suzanne is a happy homemaker in her mid-thirties who has feared flying her entire life. The fact that airplanes are statistically safer than cars is meaningless to her. After all, planes do crash, though not often. It doesn't help matters that every news article she's ever seen on the subject has been permanently imprinted on her brain. This has only solidified her belief that crashes happen more often than in fact they do.

Suzanne is an intelligent woman. She actually uses her intellect to rationalize her fear of flying. "Are several tons of steel supposed to fly through the air?" she asks. She reasons that even if there is only one chance in a million that a plane will crash, it will be hers that ends up in a crater. She feels this way even though no one in her family has a flying phobia. In fact, her parents and siblings all enjoy flying.

Because of her fear of flying, Suzanne forces her family to drive instead of flying on vacations, even though they can afford more luxurious trips. She's missed out on a few significant opportunities over the years—a trip to Aruba with friends after college graduation, the honeymoon in Greece her husband had wanted—but all in all, life has gone pretty smoothly.

Now Suzanne is being forced to confront her fear, thanks to a family wedding on the other side of the country. It's also scheduled along with her son's hockey tournament. She can't miss either one, and that means flying.

Her husband is relieved that the issue is finally being addressed. But as the days before the trip pass by, Suzanne is increasingly fearful. She's having trouble eating and sleeping. Plain and simple, she needs to change her beliefs.

CHANGE YOUR BELIEFS, CHANGE YOUR MINDSET

As in Suzanne's case, beliefs can be self-sabotaging, especially when these beliefs are bad for us or incorrect. It sometimes takes a problem or a tragedy to illuminate our knowledge to the point that we can change.

Fortunately, sometimes with education and sometimes with self-confidence, we can change our beliefs to support our goals. One way of doing this is with what is called a *submodality change technique*. This can help you discover how beliefs can be diffused and reformulated in a new way. If you can do that, you can change your mindset and your results.

Even though we have five senses—touch, smell, taste, sight, and hearing—there are only three with which we think. These are the visual, auditory, and kinesthetic senses: sight, hearing, and feeling. According to some estimates, 35 percent of us think in pictures, 25 percent of us prefer thinking in sounds, and 40 percent of us think in feelings.

I speak at conferences around the world on a topic called "People Magic." One major concept in the presentation is this very idea: that people have primary modes they think in. For example a *visual* will best remember things he saw. An *auditory* will best recall things she has heard, while a *kinesthetic* will best remember the feelings from an experience.

The U.S. military employs a very simple test to discover eye dominance in shooting a rifle. Let's try this test with you. Pick out an object in front of you on a wall. Now make a circle with your index finger and your thumb. Look through the circle to the object on the wall. Now close each eye and see which eye lines up with the object through the circle. If you can see the object with your left eye closed, you are right-eye dominant. If you could see the object with your right eye closed, you are left-eye dominant. Even though you use both eyes, one is preferred. You also have a preferred thought mode. Let's find out which mode is yours.

Think about what you experienced waking up this morning. Do you remember best what you heard, saw, or felt? When I woke up this morning, I remember looking out my bedroom window. I also remember turning on a business news channel to listen to as I stretched. I also remember how stiff I felt thanks to fifty-five years of playing tennis. But what I remember most about the first few minutes this morning is how I *felt*. Try to remember what you experienced when you woke up this morning. What sense do you remember most?

Actually, smell is the most intense sense. Your sense of smell can bring back sounds, feelings, and pictures. No other sense has this impact. One of my clients lost her mother recently. She was devastated after her mom's long illness. But it wasn't until she flew to a business meeting in Florida that the loss really hit her. A hotel room there had a smell reminiscent of her mother. It brought back intense emotions. I'm sure you have also these kinds of experiences. Some people say a song will bring them back to an event ten years ago. Or a feeling reminds them of an experience when they were a child. But smell can make even more intense memories come rushing back.

Nevertheless, it's the visual, auditory, and kinesthetic senses that we primarily use to think. You can use them to change your experiences and beliefs. To understand this technique, envision a belief you hold. Play with each pictorial difference in this belief. Try to change those characteristics in brightness, color, vividness, size, and other differences that you may notice. Make sure the belief is very specific.

For example, make your belief about future wealth into a picture of a big house in the countryside. Make your belief about becoming a better golfer into a picture of winning a major tournament in a couple of years. If your belief is that you will receive an advanced education, you might imagine a cap and gown. Use whatever represents your belief in the most visual and tangible way you can.

You can also weaken an image of a belief you want to change. Call up a picture of this belief and alter its characteristics. If your belief is large, make your picture small. If your belief is bright, make your picture dim. If it's detailed, make your picture fuzzy. If your belief is stable, make your picture flash. If your belief has color, change it to black and white. With each of these steps, notice the psychological and emotional changes you undergo.

Once you make this picture dim, small, and in black and white, you'll start to see it flash as it fades away. If you leave that frame empty with no picture to replace it, you'll experience even more anxiety. Instead, replace it with an image of a belief you want to have: You have the power to lose as many pounds as you want. You have the ability to fire a staff person who is unproductive, late, and rude. You have the power to overcome a fixed mindset of not listening to the people around you and replace it with a growth mindset, whereby you learn from everyone you meet. Weaken the image of being unable to listen, eliminate it, and then replace it with the image of you being attentive.

My friend Suzanne was able to do this. She knew she wanted to overcome her fear of flying. She began by envisioning the belief that she and her husband would have a wonderful time on the coast of Maine watching their niece get married, and celebrating with her sister and relatives. She imagined the lobster boil on the eve of the wedding. She made that picture bright, vivid, and large. She was so successful at conjuring up the experience of eating fresh New England clam chowder that her mouth watered.

Then she called up the belief she wanted to change: the belief that her plane would crash. Initially, this belief was bright, vivid, and large in her mind. She deliberately changed the characteristics of the picture, making it dim, fuzzy, flashing away in the distance. She replaced that picture with a new belief: that her plane would safely and successfully take off, fly, and land on the ground.

In her mind, she saw the airplane soaring gracefully through the sky. She saw herself smiling, holding her husband's hand, and accepting peanuts from a gracious flight attendant. She actually felt the plane landing on the ground, bumping gently, and then rolling to a halt. She saw herself walking down the steps of the plane and collecting her luggage.

Suzanne was getting close to successfully changing her beliefs, but she wasn't quite there yet. The next step of the submodality change technique is to frame the new belief, not in terms of an end result, but in terms of the process that will help you achieve and gain your goal. For Suzanne, this meant seeing herself able to fly without anxiety and traveling to places around the world she had always dreamt about.

HOW TO USE THE EMOTIONAL STABILITY CHECK

The last step of the submodality change technique is to do an *emotional stability check*. Determine if there's any way your new belief could be a problem for you. Could it cause you any emotional conflict in the future? In Suzanne's case, she may fear that flying more and traveling may take her away from loved ones she cherishes. Perhaps traveling more would not be something she would enjoy in the long term. In other words, just because you are able to eliminate a fear doesn't mean you should do it. I may be able to eliminate a fear of bungee jumping, but that doesn't mean I should engage in that activity. In short, you don't need to be confident about everything. Some apprehension is good. It keeps you learning and focused. As with the blind discus thrower in a crowded stadium, the fans stay attentive.

If a new belief is good for you, then proceed. If you're not sure, use another concept, called *congruency*. It's incredibly effective in helping you decide whether a belief is emotionally good for you.

Congruency allows you to evaluate a new belief from all three thought processes—seeing, hearing, and feeling—to determine if it will create any inner conflict or anxiety for you. For example, if your new belief is to be more assertive when people are taking advantage, you might see yourself responding differently. As you plug into the three neurolinguistic thought processes, you'll see yourself as tough and assertive. That could mean the way you stand, or walk, or even the way you sit. Auditorily, you'll hear yourself talking in a very assertive way. Kinesthetically, you'll feel more confidence and greater strength in your communications with people. You'll be more assertive in letting others know how you feel.

On the other hand, if your boss is uncomfortable with you being more assertive, you might want to avoid acting this way with her. A compromise might be to weaken the current belief that you need to be assertive with everyone, and instead limit your assertiveness to people who take advantage of you.

Let's try the whole thing from the beginning. Start with a belief about a goal that on some level you doubt you can achieve or sustain.

Let's take, for example, the goal of pursuing a law degree. Your belief could be that the material will be too demanding, or that you're too old. As you look at that belief, you should try to turn it into doubt by testing each mode of thought. Try to make it small, dim, and fuzzy. Any sounds connected with it should become soft, then inaudible, and you should also turn down the strength of your feelings about it, perhaps by using the disassociation technique we discussed earlier.

Use the submodality change technique to weaken the doubt you feel. Turn the image of your learning difficulty into a flashing picture. When the flashing begins, immediately replace it with a picture of successfully studying and concentrating on the information in front of you. Most of us feel doubt based on a fixed mindset of not being smart, strong, or good-looking enough. But we often don't have the same doubt about whether we can work enough or try hard enough.

See yourself smiling while you are reading a book, as you gain new and useful information. This would be a more positive representation than thinking about whether you have enough talent. Bring the image to the forefront and make it vivid, colorful, and detailed. Notice how the frame of the picture gets bigger, and the image gets brighter and sharper. You might hear soft classical or jazz music in the background.

Notice the physiological changes you experience. You should be smiling, feeling more joyous, more encouraged, and happier about your goal. You should feel as if a load has been lifted from your mind. This is for one very good reason: two strong, conflicting beliefs about the same thing can't exist. You just have to weaken one belief before the other one can replace it. This technique simply short-circuits the process of eliminating nonsupportive beliefs and doubts.

Now frame the new belief. To develop a Results-Focused Mindset telling you that you can earn a law degree, see yourself as able to learn, possessing a great memory, and being a fast reader. When the going gets tough, refer to this mental picture. It will reinforce the Results-Focused Mindset that you need in order to carry on.

Lastly, do an emotional stability check on your new belief. If need be, use the technique of congruency to evaluate your new belief from all three thought processes, seeing, hearing, and feeling. For gaining the confidence to pursue a law degree, you would imagine what the degree looks like, sounds like, and feels like, while at the same time making sure that being a lawyer is congruent with how you feel.

I have a good friend who doesn't like being a lawyer. If he were to pursue more education for a new law specialty, no matter how he was able to change his beliefs, it wouldn't change the fact that he doesn't enjoy practicing law. Congruency means that your beliefs have to be congruent with what you enjoy and love already—as well as with what you *don't* enjoy. Bottom line: make sure the things you want to be self-confident about are in line with the things you really want.

You can also try simply replacing nonsupportive beliefs and doubts with supportive beliefs. You can do this by, first, moving from a belief to doubt; second, by contrasting the two; and third, by finally testing the new belief. Say you're good with people, and believe that as a personnel manager you could effectively help your coworkers be more productive. You might represent this by seeing an image of yourself working side by side with one employee and then with another, giving directions that will help develop win-win situations for all of you.

Now think of a doubt. Suppose your desired outcome is to become a department head in your company. But in spite of how good you are with people, you have a fixed mindset. You're afraid you don't have the ability to lead thirty individuals. How would this be represented in your mind? It might be a picture of you acting confused and disorganized, not knowing what to do next.

Look at the differences between your pictures of belief and doubt. Notice the changes in brightness, vividness, color, fuzziness. Notice how big each picture is, and whether it flashes.

Next, test each of these submodality differences, one at a time, to discover which is the most powerful in changing the doubt picture to one of belief. Perhaps going from a vivid to a dim picture has the greatest power over the doubt. Perhaps changing the color of the picture from bright primary tones to a dull gray does the trick and causes the doubt picture to flash or even fade away. Any one of the characteristics could work; you just have to test each one.

Finally, make sure you have a new belief in your mind to replace the doubt with. If you doubt your ability to become a good manager, you need to replace that doubt with a new belief that you will make whatever effort it takes to hit that goal. See yourself learning ideas and concepts quickly. Make an image of yourself flying through books that seem complex to others. As you do this, remember to think of the new belief in positive terms *only*. Also, think of the belief as a process rather than as a goal—or as a delusion. A delusion would be having the belief that you can be wealthy and then seeing yourself as the richest person in the world.

The process of changing beliefs is very simple. Through the coming days, test your new beliefs to make sure that the emotions and associations connected with them are consistent with the changes that have occurred. Do this by testing the visual representation of each of your beliefs. What does your belief look like after several days? Is it still vivid? Is it still big, colorful, and in the center of the picture frame? Does it still have all the characteristics that were there when you made it? You might have to reinforce it by going through these exercises again, but with practice you'll find the new belief integrated into your way of life.

Just remember that beliefs and goals need to be in harmony. If they are, you'll be able to work miracles, the way the great violinist Itzhak Perlman did when one of the strings on his violin broke at the beginning of a concert. It is an incredible reminder of how powerful beliefs can be.

On November 18, 1995, Itzhak Perlman came on stage to give a concert at Avery Fisher Hall at Lincoln Center in New York City. If you've ever been to a Perlman concert, you know that getting on stage is no small achievement for him. He was stricken with polio as a child, so he has braces on both legs and walks with the aid of two crutches. To see him walk across the stage one step at a time is an awesome sight. He walks painfully, yet majestically, until he reaches his chair. Then he slowly sits down, puts his crutches on the floor, undoes the clasps on his legs, tucks one foot back, and extends the other foot forward. Then he bends down and picks up the violin, puts it under his chin, nods to the conductor, and proceeds to play.

The audience was used to this ritual. This night they sat quietly while he made his way across the stage to his chair. They remained reverently silent while he undid the clasps on his legs. They waited until he was ready to play.

But this time, something went wrong. Just as he finished the first few bars, one of the strings on his violin broke. You could hear it snap—it went off like gunfire across the room. There was no mistaking what that sound meant or what he had to do. People who were there that night said, "We figured he would have to get up, put on the clasps again, pick up the crutches, and limp his way off stage, to either find another violin or else find another string for this one."

But he didn't. Instead he waited a moment, closed his eyes, and then signaled the conductor to begin again. The orchestra began, and he played from where he had left off. And he played with such passion and such power and such purity as they had never heard before.

Of course, everyone knows it is impossible to play a symphonic work with just three strings. I know that and you know that, but that night, Itzhak Perlman refused to know that. You could see him modulating, changing, and recomposing the piece in his head. At one point, it sounded as if he were changing the tuning of the strings to get new sounds from them that they had never made before.

When he finished, there was an awesome silence in the room. And then people rose and cheered. An extraordinary outburst of applause emanated from every corner of the auditorium. People were all on their feet, screaming and cheering, doing everything they could to show how much they appreciated what he had done.

He smiled, wiped the sweat from his brow, raised his bow to quiet the audience, and then said, not boastfully, but in a quiet, pensive, reverent tone, "You know, sometimes it is the artist's task to find out how much music you can still make with what you have left."

Beliefs are powerful. Use the positive beliefs you have and change those that are self-sabotaging to achieve ever greater self-confidence in your life.

Here are some assignments to help you put your new Results--Focused Mindset to work:

1. Take one of the goals and outcomes you wrote down earlier, and list both the positive and negative beliefs that either limit or empower you to achieve that goal and outcome. Then replace each of the old non-supportive beliefs with new beliefs that will support your goals. Use the submodality change technique to do this.

2. Write down three of your beliefs that are based on future hopes and expectations. Put a checkmark next to those beliefs that would support you in achieving a goal you have set for yourself. Then perform the belief check we've already outlined. What do you already believe about your abilities to achieve your goal? What part are you anxious about?

I played a tennis tournament recently at my club. One of my friends told me that there is a definite home-court advantage in tennis. I couldn't imagine that could be true, because there are no stadiums full of fans as there are in college football; there are only the friends and relatives that each player brings to the match. My friend said that most people will lose while visiting another club, because they believe it will be tougher to win. They create a fixed mindset telling them they will lose. In this case, the belief doesn't support the goal. Tennis players must believe that they can win, or they have already lost.

If your goal is to get an MBA, a belief that would support that goal might be a mindset that you're able to learn quickly, put in the effort, and desire to gain knowledge. If your goal is to earn enough money to buy a house, your belief might be that you will hit your goals every month to save money without living paycheck to paycheck. So developing a new Results-Focused Mindset is easier that you think.

LEARNED HELPLESSNESS

A major part of developing a growth mindset depends on how optimistic you are. There are several researchers who have done exhaustive study on optimism. One of these researchers is Mihaly Csikszentmihalyi (pronounced "me high cheeksentmehigh"), whom I will refer to as Dr. Mihaly, since my Hungarian pronunciation is so bad. The other is Martin Seligman, the father of a concept called *learned helplessness*. Dr. Mihaly is a professor of psychology at Claremont Graduate University in California, and Dr. Seligman is a professor of psychology at the University of Pennsylvania.

Dr. Mihaly once said that when people restrain themselves out of fear, their lives are by necessity diminished. But his theories have gone dramatically beyond the issue of fear. In his book *Flow: The Psychology of Optimal Experience*, Dr. Mihaly researched the mental state of complete concentration and absorption when doing a highly desirable activity, which he calls *flow*. In this state, people are so involved in the activity that nothing else seems to matter. The idea of flow is very close to the feeling you might get being "in the zone" or "in a groove." Dr. Mihaly calls it "the state of intrinsic motivation," where someone is totally immersed in what they are doing. This is a feeling everyone gets at some point, characterized by great absorption, engagement, and fulfillment, as well as skill.

In one magazine interview, Dr. Mihaly described flow as complete involvement in an activity for its own sake. Anxiety totally falls away. Time flies. Every action, movement, and thought follows from the previous one, like playing jazz. Your whole being is involved in your effort and skill, to your utmost ability.

The great tennis player Pete Sampras displayed flow in a semifinal match at the U.S. Open, a year before he retired in 2002. He was in a heated competition against the great Spanish player Alex Corretja. During a tiebreaker in the second set, it became very apparent that Sampras was sick. In fact after one point, he threw up on court against the back wall. There was no way he could finish the match. The whole crowd thought that he would default, giving his opponent a window to his first championship finals. But like all great champions, Sampras rallied back and won the tiebreaker. He then eked out a third-set victory, opening the way to the finals match. This describes Dr. Mihaly's flow concept dramatically. If Pete had not been in a perfect state of flow, he would have felt pain and nausea, and the debilitating effects of headache and fever. He could have defaulted on the match.

Dr. Mihaly called this flow state an *autotelic experience*: it is something that you seek for its own sake rather than as a means to something else. To achieve a flow state, a balance must be struck between the challenge of the task and the skill of the performer. If the task is too easy or too difficult, flow can't occur. The level of skill and challenge must both be *matched* and *high*. If the skill and challenge are low and matched, there is boredom. If I play tennis against a beginner, my skill level is high, but the challenge level is low, so there is no flow state. But if I play tennis against twenty-year-old touring pros, with my sixty-something body, my skill level is too low and the challenge level is too great. I could never reach flow, because, again, both skill and challenge must be matched and high.

Say you're a salesperson who has been working on a project for months. The prospect suddenly says yes. As you do the paperwork, a flow state occurs. That last interview would feel the same if it lasted ten minutes or three hours, because you are in flow. In a golf match, you hit a drive off the tee farther than you have ever hit. It sails 320 yards. Then you nail your fairway shot to the middle of the green.

You sink a one put, for a birdie. You have achieved a flow state. The hole took fifteen minutes, but felt like one. This is flow.

The great basketball star Michael Jordan was about to shoot a three-pointer in game seven against the Utah Jazz. It was the NBA finals, and if Jordan could sink the shot with three seconds left, the Chicago Bulls would win another championship. The problem was that Jordan was sick that day (like Pete Sampras), throwing up during halftime. He didn't even play much in the second half. But for that one critical shot, he was in a flow state.

Flow is a critical concept in a Results-Focused Mindset. If your skill level is much greater than the challenge, you will get bored. If the challenge is much greater than your skill, your mindset will be undermined, as you will feel tremendous anxiety. A good example is giving a speech. You know your material, but have only done it in front of small groups of fifteen to twenty. Your skill level is high, but the challenge is low, so there is no flow. But when you speak in front of two thousand people, not only do you have to know the material, you have to entertain them in order to keep their attention. A greater skill level is demanded because the challenge is so high. If you don't possess enough skill to be brilliant in front of two thousand people instead of just fifteen, flow will be replaced by stress and anxiety. You can develop your speaking skills by rehearsing and working harder. You can also improve your skills by working with a speech coach.

So you see, it is not enough to push yourself to do an activity; you must also have the skill level to match. So you would practice the speech many times, work on putting the right stories and jokes in the right places. You would deliver it to large groups before your keynote to two thousand people. With every practice session, your belief would increase. Your mindset would develop, telling you that you had the stamina and work ethic to succeed. Your chance of achieving flow would be much greater.

One other research finding from Dr. Mihaly is *intrinsic motivation*. He found that intrinsically motivated people—that is, people who are motivated by the joy, and challenge, of doing the task itself— were more likely to be goal-oriented and directed. These are precisely the kinds of people who enjoy challenges, leading to an increase in overall happiness. According to Dr. Mihaly, intrinsic motivation is a very powerful trait. It can optimize and enhance positive experience, feelings, and overall well-being.

This means that you should challenge yourself constantly with a Results-Focused Mindset. Challenge yourself in sports, your job, family life, and every other area of your life. People with a fixed mindset tend to avoid situations in which they can't perform well. They employ avoidance behaviors like saying, "I'm too tired," "I don't want to do it because I'm not that good," or "I don't have time" when they feel that the goal isn't worth the effort. But the research on intrinsic motivation suggests that just trying new things, whether you perform well or not, will increase your feeling of well-being and self-confidence. This is the essence of the Results-Focused Mindset.

Martin Seligman's concept of learned helplessness is equally useful. Simply put, it means that once we fail at an activity, we often learn to avoid that same action in the future, because we have learned to never succeed at it. This is one of the ways a fixed mindset starts. "I have tried that before, and it didn't work. Why make the same mistake again?"

Designer Coco Chanel once said, "Success is most often achieved by those who don't know that failure is inevitable." In a Results-Focused Mindset, the premise would be, "I have had setbacks before, but through hard work, I can overcome any obstacle."

I am a researcher turned business psychologist. I still love to discuss the actual experiments used to develop concepts like learned helplessness. In one group, dogs were put in harnesses for a period of time and released. In groups 2 and 3, they were put in yoked pairs. A dog in group 2 would be intentionally subjected to painful electric shocks. But the group 2 dog could end the shocks by pressing a lever. The group 3 dog was wired in series with the group 2 dog, receiving electrical shocks of identical intensity and duration. But lever for the group 3 dog did not stop the electric shocks, no matter how many times it was pushed. To the group 3 dog, it seemed that the shocks ended at random, because it was his paired dog, in group 2, that caused the pain to stop. The group 1 and group 2 dogs quickly recovered from the experience, but the group 3 dogs learned to be helpless. They also showed symptoms similar to chronic clinical depression.

In another experiment, Seligman and his associate, Steven F. Maier, used three groups of dogs in a shuttle-box apparatus, in which the dogs could escape electric shocks by jumping over a low partition. Surprisingly, the group 3 dogs, which had previously learned that nothing they did had any impact on the shocks, just lay down passively and whined. Even though all they had to do was jump over a partition, they didn't even try. The researchers called this *retardation of learning*, whereby a learner gives up without trying. In a fixed-mindset world, something can't be accomplished because you don't have the talent to do it. You were told once that you weren't good at it, and you believed it. A fixed mindset was created.

One of the most interesting aspects of these experiments was what the researchers did next. They would verbally encourage the dogs to jump over the partition, and even hold treats out as an incentive. But the dogs would just lie there, unresponsive to any threat or reward. The researcher actually had to pick the helpless dog up, move its legs, and lift it over the partition, teaching it how to escape the shock. The biggest surprise was that the researcher had to do this exercise twice before the dog learned it could escape.

In a way, this research should not be surprising. I'm sure you've been to a zoo or a circus. The elephants are tethered to stakes with a very light rope. They could easily escape. But obviously this is not the first time the elephants have been tethered. When an elephant is a baby, one of its legs is chained to a metal stake. No matter what the baby does, escape is futile. Gradually the elephant learns that anything around its leg, fastened to any structure, is also inescapable. This is learned helplessness.

Golf is one of the most difficult sports I've ever played. Of course, tennis is hard as well. But after nearly fifty-eight years of playing tennis, both as an amateur and a pro, I am confident of playing well or, as my body gets older, at least of having fun. Golf is a different story. I never know which Kerry Johnson will show up— the Kerry Johnson with a tee shot in the middle of the fairway, or the Kerry Johnson who shanks into the parking lot. The only way to mitigate mistakes is to practice a lot. If I'm in town, I play two rounds a week. But I practice at the driving range at least three times a week.

One of my best friends, Mark, refuses to play golf with me. It isn't that he *can't* play, it's that he *won't*. Five years ago, Mark, I, and a couple other friends played at Pelican Hills Golf Club in Newport Beach, California. As a tennis player, Mark has great hand and eye coordination. He was able to transfer that athleticism somewhat to the golf course. At Pelican Hills, he shot a 105. Not a bad score. Only 5 percent of the golfers in America shoot below 100. So Mark thinks he is worse than he really is. The last time I asked Mark to play golf in front of some friends, he said, "I can't play golf. I tried it, and it was ugly." I know Mark enjoyed our last round. I also know that he can play, though not well. But the fact that he refuses because he's not good enough is another example of learned helplessness.

What are some activities you have tried that didn't work, so you never tried them again? Have you avoided starting an MBA because you once failed a math course? Have you refused sales training because you were rejected on the phone once twenty years ago? Have you avoided working with a business coach because the last one didn't help? Learned helplessness can have an impact on many aspects of your business and personal life.

In one experiment with babies, a sensory pillow was used that could control the rotation of a mobile above the crib. If the baby moved its head to one side, the mobile would rotate, while movement to the other side would stop the mobile. Another group of babies was put into cribs which also had mobiles above their heads, but with no sensory pillow. Both sets of babies were later given sensory pillows that had full control over the rotation of the mobiles. But only the babies who learned to control the mobile previously attempted to use it to control the mobile again. Obviously the first group of babies learned to control the mobile, and the second group of babies learned to be helpless.

Several of my friends are ex–US Navy SEALs. I have already mentioned that the Basic Underwater Demolition School, or BUDS, is dramatic, excruciating, and more challenging than any in the military. Not only are the SEALs subjected to ice-cold water for hours at a time, they are given one or two hours of sleep per night, for weeks on end. Much of this is an attempt to weed out the less dedicated recruits. But one concept the trainers use is to teach the BUDS how to escape from learned helplessness. Of course the Navy doesn't call it learned helplessness; they call it *unfairness*. While the candidates are out on evening exercises, trainers will go in the barracks and take sheets off a couple of beds. After eighteen hours of training, the candidates are so exhausted they can barely walk. As they enter the barracks, an inspection is announced, with the trainers looking for violations. Of course the trainers target the beds without sheets and punish the candidates who are not in compliance. While this sounds totally unfair and reprehensible to us, it teaches the candidates that unfairness will occur and needs to be overcome. These candidates will have to accept their fate and spend the rest of the night without sleep as punishment. But the real lesson is that, even in the face of learned helplessness, they learn to overcome obstacles.

These findings are very important for developing your own Results-Focused Mindset for attempting new activities. If you have failed at something in the past, you may have learned that it's futile to attempt it again in the future. As I mentioned earlier, I was cut by my JV basketball team coach at sixteen years old. Unlike some superstars, like Michael Jordan, who was also cut from his high-school basketball team, I never played competitive basketball again, even though nearly all my friends played. I rationalized that I liked tennis, baseball, football, and golf a lot more. I'm not saying that coaches shouldn't cut weaker players. But we all should be aware of our tendencies to give up and learn to be helpless. Just because you failed at something before doesn't mean you can't learn to do it effectively in the future.

A navy captain is alerted by his first mate that there is a pirate ship coming towards his position. He asks a sailor to get him his red shirt.

The captain is asked, "Why do you need a red shirt?"

He replies, "So that when I bleed, you guys don't notice and aren't discouraged." They eventually fight off the pirates.

The next day, the captain is alerted that fifty pirate ships are coming towards their boat. He yells, "Get me my brown pants!"

Here are some stories of people who have overcome learned helplessness.

- Walt Disney was once fired from his job at a newspaper for "lacking ideas." He had also had several bankruptcies and had been turned down by over a hundred banks before he developed Disneyland.

- Vince Lombardi was told by an expert that he "possesses minimal football knowledge. Lacks motivation."

- Clarence Birdseye discovered the secret of flash freezing, which turned out to create the entire frozen-food industry. This only happened after he went bankrupt seven times.

- Bob Parsons is the founder and CEO of GoDaddy.com, a hugely successful registrar of web domain names. If you read his blog postings (on bobparsons.com), you'll see that he overcame a lot in pursuit of his dream. He was definitely not an overnight success and experienced a lot of failure on the way. But he kept his vision in his mind at all times and said, "I spent very little time looking back or feeling sorry for myself." Another awesome quote from Parsons is, "Quitting is easy. The easiest thing to do in the world is to quit and give up on your dreams (and quite frankly, that's what all the non–risk takers want you to do)."

- A teacher of the great Ludwig van Beethoven once told him he was a hopeless composer.

- Colonel Harland Sanders, creator of Kentucky Fried Chicken, was told "no" by over a thousand restaurants for more than a year while he lived out of his car trying to sell his chicken recipe.

As I have mentioned before it's very difficult to change to a Results-Focused Mindset. We can all learn and grow, but changing who we are and our core personality is nearly impossible. You're probably thinking right now, why even hear about developing a better mindset, if I can't change? But you *can* learn. The difficulty is in the follow-up and in the courage and discipline to execute what you know.

THE RESOURCE CIRCLE

One technique for dealing with anxiety and learned helplessness involves using a *resource circle*. Simply concentrate on a time or an event in which you were completely successful. The event could be winning a sporting contest, or giving a brilliant speech, or receiving an award. In your mind, draw an imaginary circle on the floor or ground next to you. Now try to access that past event. Try to see it. Try to hear the sounds around you as if you were there, and try to invoke the feelings you experienced when the event originally happened.

When you believe you are as close as possible to reliving the event, take a step into that imaginary circle. Then step out and repeat the exercise, recalling the event as it sounded, looked, and felt at the time. Now do it again without using the three senses. Just step right into the circle. You should be able to immediately access that same winning feeling just by stepping into the circle. This is called a *resource state*.

I recently spoke to a man who told me he felt horrible about being overweight, but his patience and his belief in himself had come to an end. He was stressed. He remembered the resource-circle technique, mentally drew his circle on the ground, and stepped into it. Not only did his stress level go down, but he was able to strengthen his positive belief and mindset. He controlled his anxiety and reached his weight-loss goal.

The most powerful coaches, business people, athletes, professionals and scientists are those who, on cue and largely unconsciously, put themselves into powerful resource states by accessing an effective mindset. Many are able to do this in spite of horrible things that occur in their lives, whether it's ill health, financial breakdown, family problems, or other tragedies. They can keep themselves in a successful resource state by triggering powerful mechanisms in their minds. A resource circle is a state of mind you can step into to access a resource state. A resource state can also be accessed by an action like watching a motivation video of listening to a inspirational lecture.

Often before a football game, NFL players will pound each other on the shoulder pads. I thought this was a way to check the pads until I learned about resource circles. But the fastest way in which players get motivated and put themselves into a winning mindset is the chanting they do in circles before a game. New Orleans Saints quarterback Drew Brees is one of the only quarterbacks who leads this type of chant. It whips the team up so fast and so well that they are one of the fastest teams out of the starting block in the NFL. You can also use resources states to create your own mindset, just as NFL players do.

One resource state I used as a pro tennis player was the way I bounced the ball before a serve. I would bounce it exactly two times before a first serve and only once before a second serve. You might think this is just superstition, but I could put myself into a confident mindset with this simple act. Pro tennis player Rafael Nadal uses his own resource state. He tucks his hair behind both ears before serving. Is this superstition or resource state? As a TV beer commercial once said, "It's only superstition if it doesn't work."

ATTACHMENT

One additional technique you can use to control anxiety is called *attachment*. Attachment is a way to attach a different attitude or even a mindset to an activity. It's a way of attaching positive emotions to an activity. Many athletes with performance anxiety use attachment to compete at their best. For example, before beginning a race, a sprinter will put her hands on her hips, to access past relaxation or a past success, before kneeling down to the starting blocks. A 400-meter dash is an enormously stressful endeavor. Many racers lose before they start with huge expenditures of anxiety in the minutes leading up to the race. But when an athlete can put her hands on her hips and calm herself down, she can gain control and put herself in a position to win. This is another example of accessing a resource state.

5

How to Use Meta-Patterns

One day the father in a wealthy family took his son on a trip to the country with the firm purpose of showing him how poor some people are. They spent a couple of days and nights on the farm of a very poor family.

On their return home, the father asked his son, "Well, what do you think of that family?"

"They were great, Dad," his son replied.

"Did you see how poor some people are?" the father asked.

"Oh, yes," said the son.

"So what did you learn from the trip?" asked the father.

The son answered, "I learned that we have one dog, and they have four. We have a pool that reaches to the middle of our yard, and they have a creek that has no end. We have imported lanterns in our garden, and they have all the stars in heaven. We have a small piece of land to live on, and they have fields that go beyond our sight. We have servants who take care of us, but they serve others. We buy our food, but they grow theirs. We have walls around our property to protect us, but they have friends to protect them."

With this the boy's father was speechless.

Then his son added, "Thanks, Dad, for showing me how poor
we are."

The father in the story above had a Results-Focused Mindset. The life
of a farm family was "poor." The life of a family living in the lushness
of a city with all that money could buy was "rich." This man's mindset was that his perceptions weren't necessarily accurate—until his
son stunned him with the how he perceived the difference between
the rich life of the family on the farm and the poorer life in the city.
The father's perception and mindset changed. Mindset is a culmina-
tion of how you perceive the world, or your *meta-patterns*.

WHAT ARE META-PATTERNS?

Meta-patterns are really an explanation of how we humans process
information. They are like an internal computer program that allows
us either to pay attention to or ignore certain bits of information that
can affect our attitudes and perceptions. Meta-patterns are the states
of mind we automatically access as we work to achieve what we want
out of life.

Once upon a time, an exasperated mother whose son was always
getting into mischief finally asked him, "How do you expect to get
into heaven?"

The boy thought it over and said, "Well, I'll just run in and out
and in and out and keep slamming the door until St. Peter says, 'For
heaven's sake, Jimmy, come in or stay out!'"

Jimmy, like most children, had a mindset influenced by his
meta-patterns. The two can be closely linked. When my daughter
Caroline was eight years old, she found that she couldn't compete

with her older sister, Catherine, then ten, either intellectually or physically. But she did have other resources: she could cry and whine. When she wanted something or felt her sister was taking advantage, she would do a sort of combined cry/whine that was very effective in helping her get what she wanted. After all, Mom and Dad always came running.

Catherine also found a behavior that worked in helping her get her way: aggression. When she wanted something, Catherine would just take it from her sister, which in turn caused Caroline to again do the cry/whine.

Getting into mischief, crying/whining, and resorting to aggression are just three of the meta-patterns kids commonly use. Adults use meta-patterns too, though less often than children. And adult meta-patterns are more complex.

Meta-patterns are more than preferences. They're the drives that keep us moving in a certain direction, whether it's toward or away from something. Some of us move toward heavy physical exercise, for example, spending time in gyms or outdoors jogging or walking. Others move away from strenuous physical activity. Still others move towards the arts by going to concerts, museums, or the ballet, while others shun everything except hoedowns in the barn.

Human beings display five types of meta-patterns. Knowing what they are, how they influence your behaviors and belief, will help you develop the mindset you want.

META-PATTERN ONE: MOVING TOWARD OR AWAY

If somebody asked you what you wanted out of your career, your family, or your life, would you tell them what you wanted or what you didn't want? Likewise, does your cup tend to be half full or half empty? This tendency to move toward or away makes up the first type of meta-patterns.

Someone with a *moving toward* meta-pattern would answer the question in terms of what they *want*. Someone with a *moving away* meta-pattern would answer the question in terms of what they *don't* want.

My wife, Merita, will ask me where I want to go to dinner. I will give her three options, to which she always says no. When I ask where she wants to eat, she will usually reply, "I don't care. Any place you want."

To determine whether your meta-state is one of moving toward or away, think about how you tend to answer the typical question asked when you get home from work or school: "How was your day?" If your tendency is to answer "Great!" or some such variation, your meta-state is one of moving toward. If your tendency is to answer somewhat negatively, such as "Not so good" or "OK, I guess" or "Rotten, as usual," your meta-state is one of moving away.

I'm always amazed when I ask someone how they are and hear, "Things could be worse" or "So-so," and then hear others say, "Great!" or "Couldn't be better." Recognize the meta-patterns of moving toward and moving away here?

You can also ask yourself how you decided to buy or rent your last home. Respond out loud if you can. If you answer that you decided on your current home because it had a beautiful view with a big yard or old graceful trees or something else positive, your meta-state is one of moving toward an option. If you answer it was the best of a bad lot or you liked it at first but wouldn't move there again because the living room is too small, your meta-state is one of moving away.

Or ask yourself how you decided to buy your last car. If you answer that it was the only one you could afford, your meta-state is one of moving away. If you describe all the great things about it, your meta-state is one of moving toward.

Recently I asked a friend what she desired from a date. She spent almost half an hour telling me what she didn't want in a man. She didn't want someone who was poor, who wasn't able to show her attention, who didn't spend a lot of time with her, and who wasn't tall, dark, and handsome. I understood what she didn't want, but I was still confused about what she did want. I even asked her the same question again. It was interesting that she said, "I just told you, didn't I?"

META-PATTERN TWO: FRAME OF REFERENCE

The second meta-pattern that makes up our attitude is our *frame of reference*. This frame of reference is either *internal* or *external*. For example, how do you know when you've done a good job on a project? If you know you've done well only when others tell you that you have, your frame of reference is *external*. If you have a gut feeling that your work is good no matter what anyone says, your frame of reference is *internal*. Pretty self-explanatory, isn't it?

I was thinking about beginning my MBA program a few years back when a friend said, "Are you nuts? You already have a PhD. You are really successful. You won't have as much time at home to spend with your wife and kids. This is crazy; the time it will take you to study won't be worth it." Can you hear the fixed mindset in this guy?

This reaction really threw me, and for a time I didn't enter the program. If you have an external frame of reference, other people can knock you off a Results-Focused Mindset. If you have an internal frame of reference, you are more likely to stay focused on your goal.

To be more results-focused, we all need to have a greater *internal* frame of reference. To strengthen your internal frame, once you've set an outcome for yourself, measure every action you take against that outcome. This will help you resist external forces that might draw you away from it.

Another way to strengthen your internal frame of reference is to use the belief representations we talked about earlier. Try right now to reaccess that picture of the belief that supports an outcome you have in mind.

For instance, if you're working on that MBA, imagine yourself breezing through graduate studies at the top of your class. Try to pay very close attention to the brightness, the size, and the vividness of the picture. Now go back to thinking about your outcome: getting the MBA. That outcome will occur if you stay internally focused. Then, every time you hear doubting comments, call to mind the picture of the belief that shows you have the ability to get that MBA.

META-PATTERN THREE: SORTING

The third meta-pattern involves how emotions are *sorted*. This basically concerns how we see ourselves in relation to others. If you sort only by yourself, you might be a self-absorbed, arrogant, fixed-mindset egotist. On the other hand, if you consistently sort by others, you might be an emotional martyr.

How does this meta-pattern of sorting affect developing a better mindset? As in the case of the external or internal frame of reference, if you sort by others exclusively, your meta-pattern may sabotage your chances of staying in a Results-Focused Mindset and remaining focused on your objectives and outcomes.

For example, I knew a man who consistently shot himself in the foot trying to build a successful company. He was a victim of how much he sorted by others. Warren Harvey was brilliant and a hard worker. He was also a well-liked, generous man who could be counted on to quietly slip you a twenty-dollar bill from his pocket or buy you lunch at the local café if you were on hard times.

His dream was to own his own real-estate company, and by the time he was forty years old, he had achieved this dream. Times were good, business was booming, and Harvey had soon employed a dozen or so support staff, and had taken on a number of partners, individuals whose company he greatly enjoyed and who also desired great wealth.

Unfortunately, even though the new employees and partners were pleasant people to work with, not all of them had Harvey's brilliance or work ethic. When the economy took a nosedive and the real-estate market fell off, Harvey worked harder than ever and continued to bring money into the company. But the money he brought in just went to support all the various staff who were not earning their own keep. It did not go into Harvey's pocket (though he spent money as if it did).

The years went by, and the pattern continued. It wasn't long before Harvey had dug himself into a financial hole so deep that his wife had to go to work to help support the family. Twenty years later, she's still working to help extricate the family from debt, while Harvey's business goes on much the same as before, employing numerous staff who cost a lot and who bring in very little money, with Harvey working endless hours and bringing in just enough to keep them all going. Ironically, closing up shop and working for himself alone would bring him a level of wealth that would keep him quite comfortable, but he can't bring himself to do it. He feels responsible for all these people he's employed and doesn't want to let them down.

While the story of Warren Harvey might make it look like sorting by self is best, the best of both worlds is to be somewhere in the middle, leaning toward the side of sorting by self. You can't and shouldn't ignore others, but it's important to keep focused on your own goals and outcomes.

The biblical story of Job is a good example. Satan challenged God, saying that his servant Job was only loyal because of the great blessings God bestowed. God took his blessings away and allowed Satan to make Job's life a living hell. Job's children died, his wealth vanished, and Job was stricken with the most miserable illnesses a human could have. Job's wife told him to curse God. But Job stayed loyal to God, proving he was truly God's servant, and not just because of God's blessings. Job's wealth was restored, and he eventually had more children. If Job had been sorting by self, he would have defined his self-worth solely by what he had. But since he sorted by his relationship to God, he was able to survive the misfortunes he had to endure.

Here are some questions to determine whether you sort by others or by self: what do you like best about your job? If you answer that it pays well or the hours are good or give another self-oriented reason, you are sorting by self. On the other hand, if you like your job because you enjoy meeting new people, you probably sort by others.

Likewise, do you like to work with others or by yourself? If you answer "by yourself," you probably sort by self. The opposite is true if you work best with others. Just remember that sorting by others can harm your efforts in hitting your goals. If you sort by others, they may discourage you from maintaining a Results-Focused Mindset. After all, if you have a deadline to get a project done, but someone questions why and says it's not that important, sorting by others doesn't help.

META-PATTERN FOUR: NECESSITY OR POSSIBILITY

The fourth meta-pattern that affects our attitude is the tendency to be motivated by *necessity* or *possibility*. Here is a heartwarming story about a little girl with a Results-Focused Mindset and who is clearly motivated by possibility rather than necessity:

> *Sarah, ten years old, wears a brace all the time because she was born with a muscle missing in her left foot. She came home one beautiful spring day to tell her father she had just competed in field day at school, where they have lots of races and other competitive events.*
>
> *Because of her leg support, her father's mind raced as he tried to think of encouragement for Sarah, things he could say to her about not letting this get her down. Before he could get a word out, she said, "Daddy, I won two of the races!"*
>
> *Her father couldn't believe it! And then Sarah said, "I had an advantage."*
>
> *Ah . . . The father knew it. He figured she must have been given a head start or some other kind of physical advantage.*
>
> *But again, before he could say anything, Sarah said, "Daddy, I didn't get a head start. My advantage was I had to try harder!"*

A good way to discover how somebody is motivated is to ask why they bought their house. If they say they needed a five-bedroom house because they have four kids or because they needed a study to work in, they are probably motivated by necessity. Likewise, station-wagon owners and van drivers are more likely motivated by necessity than by possibility, while those driving Corvettes or Porsches are more likely motivated by possibility than necessity.

Possibility people are motivated less by what they *have* to do than by what they *want* to do. They see a wide variety of choices, experiences, and options in life. They're very interested in knowing what they *can* have rather than what they *should* have.

In terms of your mindset and your ability to work hard enough to achieve your outcomes, it's good to have a mixture of both types of motivation. Although your goals should take into account the necessities of staying committed, they should also include the meta-pattern of thinking about possibilities—looking at new ways of how you can reach your outcomes more quickly.

META-PATTERN FIVE: WORK STYLE

The fifth and last type of meta-pattern involves your particular work style. There are three kinds of work-style meta-patterns. The first is *independent*, the second is *cooperative*, and the third relates to *proximity*.

1. **Independent**. The independent meta-pattern is displayed in those who get a great deal of enjoyment from working on their own. These individuals like to work by themselves and take full credit for it. They're the sort who want less to become part of a group than to lead a group. They may have difficulty working with other people.

2. **Cooperative**. Individuals with a cooperative meta-pattern want to be part of a decision-making body. They want to share responsibilities and activities. They're the sort of people who are less likely to make decisions on their own than to get agreement from others before they commit themselves.

For example, if one of your goals is to read every evening, but your meta-pattern includes a cooperative, interpersonal mindset, you might find it difficult to spend that much time by yourself. The solution might be to read one hour each evening before joining friends.

Take another example: Every January, I go skiing with about forty doctors from around the U.S. who form the Blue River Trauma Society (BRTS). We helicopter in to the rugged mountain range in British Columbia called the Cariboos. You have to be an advanced or expert skier to attempt this kind of risky adventure, but all the docs in the group have a wonderful time. One day, one of the physicians wanted to go into the lodge because it was too cold. He complained a little and could have gone in anytime, but instead tried to get agreement from the four other people in the helicopter before he stopped for the day. It was really funny to see the cooperative meta-pattern played out in front of my eyes.

3. **Proximity**. The proximity meta-pattern is a mixture of the first two types. These people like to work with others, while maintaining control over a project. If this is your meta-pattern, your attitude might be influenced by the kinds of projects you're working on.

A good example of the proximity meta-pattern again comes from the BRTS group. The group's leader is an orthopedic surgeon named John Campbell, from Bozeman, Montana. He is both member and organizer. It is fun to watch him ride roughshod over what often looks like an ill-behaved fraternity. Yet he still revels in the group's activities.

This proximity meta-pattern seems to include the best of both worlds. You get to enjoy others' company, but you have the ability to run things or simply be by yourself.

Has this meta-pattern information begun to sink in? Let's test it and see how well you can apply it. Think about the last few U.S. presidents, beginning with Barack Obama. Which meta-patterns apply to him? Possibly an independent one: he didn't like to work with congressional leaders. My daughter, Stacey, who worked in Congress both as a PR secretary and as a chief of staff, once said that Obama wielded a phone and a pen because he had trouble working with others to get consensus.

President George W. Bush: which meta-patterns do you think he displayed? Does he seem to move toward or away from issues? This is debatable, but he seemed to move away from many divisive issues in the beginning of his presidency until terrorism took front stage. Then he moved toward it, as the old saying goes, "like white on rice."

Here's a tougher one: During Bill Clinton's scandals, do you think he sorted by himself or by others? He seemed to be watching the polls pretty carefully in the heat of his troubles, especially regarding the Monica Lewinsky issue. He also appeared to find amazing confidence after a poll showed that the American people didn't want to see him impeached merely for an extramarital affair. Right or wrong, sorting by others seems to have enabled him to weather the calls for his resignation.

Finally, do you think Ronald Reagan used an independent or proximity meta-pattern? Presidential historians tell us that he seemed to be great in front of crowds but didn't particularly like day-to-day cabinet meetings. He was also famous for leaving much of the responsibility for various governmental workings to his cabinet. In spite of this, no one has claimed he wasn't a great leader. Rather, the argument has been made that sometimes leadership is manifested in motivating large groups rather than in interactions with only a few.

It should be obvious by now that meta-patterns have a great bearing on the mindset we can develop and maintain. Because of this, either the mindset attitude and belief approaches we take need to fit well into the meta-patterns we already possess, or we need to alter our meta-patterns to accommodate the mindset we want.

The good news is, we can attempt to change our meta-patterns by distorting, deleting, or generalizing incoming information. We all do this to some extent anyway as we deal with various situations. Why not consciously capitalize on it to help develop and maintain the mindset you want? As George Bernard Shaw once said, "If you can't get rid of the skeleton in your closet, you'd best teach it to dance."

For example, if your meta-pattern is one in which you tend to sort by self, but a friend has a big office party coming up that she wants you to attend with her, you can *distort* the information that causes you anxiety by telling yourself, "I will not be the only person at this party who doesn't enjoy big get-togethers. There will be someone else hanging out in the corner or the kitchen, and I will be able to escape there too when I need a break."

In another example, say you are an individual with a moving away meta-pattern whose desired outcome is to get an MBA, and you read an article that degrees of this type are no longer as important as they once were for getting a better job. Your automatic response might be to say, "Why am I killing myself working an eight-hour job and going to class at the same time?"

Instead, *delete* this information that favors your meta-pattern and rationalize to yourself that there will always be great opportunities for qualified people, more so now than ever before.

Likewise, if you're having trouble staying on your diet, you could delete that particular bit of information and tell yourself that a little sacrifice now will be nothing compared to the joy you will have with a new body after a couple of months of dieting.

You can also *generalize* incoming information to help alter a particular meta-pattern. For example, if your frame of reference is external and your wife has a business meeting out of town for the second weekend in a row, don't tell yourself, "This really stinks! I can't believe she's leaving again so soon! Now what am I going to do?"

Instead, say to yourself, "Despite how it appears right now, this doesn't happen very often, and it means she's really doing well in the company. I'm proud of her and I know she will miss me too, but this will be a good chance for me to get some much-needed work done around the house."

It can take some time to get into the habit of working with our existing meta-patterns. Traumatic situations, though never desired, can cut through the chase and help us change our meta-patterns quickly, as the following story suggests:

> *Some time ago a man punished his five-year-old daughter for wasting a roll of expensive gold wrapping paper. Money was tight, and he became upset when the child pasted the gold paper on a box to put under the Christmas tree.*
>
> *Nevertheless, the little girl brought the gift to her father the next morning and said, "This is for you, Daddy."*
>
> *The father was embarrassed by his earlier reaction, but his anger flared again when he found the box was empty. He spoke to the child in a harsh manner. "Don't you know, young lady, that when you give someone a present there's supposed to be something inside the package?"*
>
> *The little girl looked up at him with tears in her eyes and said, "Oh, Daddy, it's not empty. I blew kisses into it until it was full."*
>
> *The father was crushed. He fell on his knees and put his arms around his little girl and begged her to forgive him for his unnecessary anger.*

An accident took the life of the child only a short time later, and it is said that the father was a changed man forever. He kept that gold box by his bed for all the remaining years of his life. Whenever he was discouraged or faced difficult problems, he would open the box and take out an imaginary kiss and remember the love of the child who had put it there.

USING META-PATTERNS SUCCESSFULLY

Regardless of which meta-patterns you display, in order to use them successfully you need to keep in mind the following four tips:

1. Recognize which meta-patterns you possess. For example, if you have a meta-pattern that's typically moving toward things, then thinking about a great body is a better way to slim down than to think about losing weight. If your meta-pattern is moving away, thinking about actually losing weight would be a more effective way for you to achieve your outcome.

2. Use your frame of reference, whether internal or external, to support your goal and outcome. For example, if your frame of reference is external, it would be a good idea to tell yourself you'd be a great candidate for a weight-loss program because of your concern about other's opinions.

3. Change your belief systems to best utilize your existing meta-patterns. As you may find, meta-patterns can be difficult to change. If your meta-pattern is one of moving toward rather than moving away and your diet outcomes are focused on losing twenty-five pounds, there's a conflict. To make your meta-patterns and outcomes congru-

ent, you can use a belief in your ability to eat two small meals a day instead of three large meals. That's a way to modify the outcome to best use the existing meta-pattern.

4. Monitor yourself through your mindset change program. Make sure you're actively focusing on information that supports your most effective meta-pattern. For example, if your frame of reference tends to be external, make sure you don't let others discourage you. If your frame of reference is internal, you may want to insulate yourself from others and not tell them what your goals are.

I tend to move away from things rather than towards them. Another of my meta-patterns is necessity rather than possibility. During the final stretch of my MBA studies, I found the course on managerial accounting so difficult that I actually asked my CPA for help. John gave me a fixed-mindset definition. He told me there are two types of people in the world: those who have a mind for numbers and those who don't. He advised me to drop out of the course until I had time to take another prerequisite, but I had invested too much time and trouble for that. Getting an A+ in the course didn't motivate me, but getting a D did. As soon as I was able to see how near I was to failing, I jumped into high gear, studying and cramming almost twelve hours a day until the final exam. I ended up with an A+ for the course, but it wasn't because I was trying to do well. I was trying not to fail. I was using a "moving away from" meta-pattern.

Knowing my meta-patterns enables me to concentrate on what is naturally appealing. For example, there are some goals in life I want to just go out and grab. These include a better serve and fore-hand in tennis. There are also some problems I want to move away from. These include traffic tickets, flight delays, and behavior problems with my kids. Likewise, I love to speak to groups, but I hate airline flights. The carriers are increasingly passenger-unfriendly, the security is tighter, and it is becoming lunacy to have to spend ninety minutes waiting to get through a security line, especially in Chicago and Newark.

It would be easy to say that my career is too tough. (Recognize the moving away meta-pattern?) Instead, I distort the airline experiences in favor of remembering the great places I travel to and the wonderful people I'm privileged to address. It helps to remember the following quote by Winston Churchill when I'm tempted to let situations and events beyond my control get to me: "A pessimist sees the difficulty in every opportunity; an optimist sees the opportunity in every difficulty."

In the final analysis, it's good to be aware of your meta-patterns for one overriding reason: you can put them to work for you instead of against you, as the young executive in the following story eventually managed to do.

A young and successful executive was traveling down a neighborhood street, as usual going a bit too fast in his new Jaguar. He loved to drive fast, loved the rush of adrenaline it gave him. He was watching for kids darting out from between parked cars and slowed down when he thought he saw something.

As his car passed, no children appeared. Instead, a brick smashed into the Jag's side door. The man slammed on the brakes and drove the Jag back to the spot where the brick had been thrown.

The angry driver then jumped out of the car, grabbed the nearest kid, and pushed him up against a parked car, shouting, "What was that all about? What the heck are you doing? That's a new car, and that brick you threw is going to cost a lot of money. Why did you do it?"

The young boy was apologetic. "Please mister . . . Please, I'm sorry. I didn't know what else to do. I threw the brick because no one would stop."

With tears dripping down his face, the youth pointed to a spot just around a parked car. "It's my brother," he said. "He rolled off the curb and fell out of his wheelchair and I can't lift him up."

Now sobbing, the boy asked the stunned executive, "Would you please help me get him back into his wheelchair? He's hurt and he's too heavy for me."

Moved beyond words, the driver tried to swallow the rapidly swelling lump in his throat. He hurriedly lifted the handicapped boy back into the wheelchair, then took out his fancy handkerchief and dabbed at the fresh scrapes and cuts. A quick look told him everything was going to be OK.

"Thank you and may God bless you," the grateful child told the stranger.

Shaken, the man simply watched the little boy push his wheelchair-bound brother down the sidewalk toward their home.

It was a long, slow walk back to the Jaguar. The damage was very noticeable, but the driver never bothered to repair the dented side door. He knew he needed to keep the dent there so he'd never forget its message: don't go through life so fast that someone has to throw a brick at you to get your attention.

Ah, meta-patterns. Thinking about what your meta-patterns are and getting into the habit of putting them to your advantage to achieve greater self-discipline may take some effort, but it's effort that will more than pay off in the long run.

Assignments: Using Meta-Patterns to Improve Your Mindset

1. Identify the five meta-patterns you display and evaluate them to see how many support the goals and outcomes that you want to pursue.

2. Think of your values and goals and try to come up with three new or modified outcomes that would fit nicely into the meta-patterns you already possess.

3. Think about the possibility of altering your meta-patterns to more successfully achieve your self-discipline goals. Is it possible to do that? What specifically would you need to do?

LOCUS OF CONTROL

Locus of control will help you understand whether your mindset is affected by external things that happen to you, or whether you are able to control your environment. Are you internally or externally controlled? Are you reactive to what happens around you?

Many sports coaches believe that repetition can help you develop a successful mindset. I think that's true. If you do something over and over again, you'll be able to develop more confidence. We aren't talking about false self-confidence—like trying to fly a 747 without any training—but rational self-confidence, when you have to put in what one of my friends calls the "hard yards." But repetition, while important, needs to be matched with goals and outcomes. (We will talk about the difference between goals and outcomes, and why experiencing a goal before you achieve it is far better than setting a goal.)

Having an inward mindset often results in anxiety and stress. Often it creates negative emotions for those participating in sporting events and stage performances, and even giving speeches. This kind of stress is called *performance anxiety*. There are four fears we feel during performance anxiety: *fear of rejection*, the *fear of looking foolish*, the *fear of failure*, and even the *fear of success*. Who would ever fear success? The problem is that many of us sabotage ourselves when we are too successful. This sounds very strange, but we will talk about how to manage and alleviate these fears.

> *There was a business executive who was deeply in debt and could see no way out. Creditors were closing in on him. Suppliers were demanding payment. He sat on the park bench, head in hands, wondering if anything could save his company from bankruptcy.*
>
> *Suddenly an old man appeared before him. "I can see that something is troubling you," he said.*
>
> *After listening to the executive's woes, the old man said, "I believe I can help you."*
>
> *He asked the man his name, wrote out a check, and pushed it into his hand saying, "Take this money. Meet me here exactly one year from today, and you can pay me back at that time."*
>
> *Then he turned and disappeared as quickly as he had come.*
>
> *The business executive saw in his hand a check for $500,000, signed by John D. Rockefeller, then one of the richest men in the world!*
>
> *"I can erase my money worries in an instant!" the executive realized. But instead he decided to put the uncashed check in his safe. Just knowing it was there might give him the strength to work out a way to save his business, he thought.*
>
> *With renewed optimism, he negotiated better deals and extended terms of payment. He closed several big sales. Within a few months, he was out of debt and making money once again.*
>
> *Exactly one year later, he returned to the park with the uncashed check. At the agreed-upon time, the old man appeared.*

But just as the executive was about to hand back the check, and share his success story, a nurse came running up and grabbed the old man.

"I'm so glad I caught him!" she cried. "I hope he hasn't been bothering you. He's always escaping from the rest home and telling people he's John D. Rockefeller."

And she led the old man away by the arm.

The executive just stood there, stunned. All year long he'd been wheeling and dealing, buying and selling, convinced he had half a million dollars behind him.

Suddenly he realized that it wasn't the money, real or imagined, that had turned his life around. It was his new-found self-confidence that had given him the power to achieve anything he went after.

That is what an effective mindset is all about. It's like knowing you have $500,000 in your pocket to save you, but knowing you will never have to cash the check. Wouldn't it be nice to have that kind of confidence?

6

Goals and Outcomes

One of the best benefits of a Results-Focused Mindset is an ability to achieve goals. Computer scientist Alan Kay once said, "The best way to predict the future is to invent it." If you know your values, you will have the ability to set goals in accordance with what you believe is important. You will minimize the conflict and discomfort in reaching those goals, because what you're working for is what you really want, your heart's desire.

But how do really successful people set goals, and how can you use a Results-Focused Mindset to hit your objectives more effectively? The answer is slicing the big goals down to manageable pieces.

SLICING

Goals may seem pretty intimidating at first. You want to achieve big things and have audacious goals, but you don't know where to start. How do you eat an elephant? One bite at a time. The technique of slicing is a big help. There are two ways to use slicing. *Slicing down* is a way to segment major concepts into smaller bits of information.

For example, breaking the category "animal" into a smaller section might mean to slice it down into "marsupials" or "fowl" or "rodents." Slicing down from the topic of "machine" might be to break the category into smaller components, like "car" or "computer."

A *slice-up* means the reverse: to expand something from a specific category into a broader one. To slice up "car" might mean expanding it to "transportation" or "trip." To slice up "anxiety" might mean to generalize into "psychological discomfort."

Slicing is important because it helps you organize your goals into a specific plan. I remember when I was in college: my goal was to earn both a PhD and an MD. But I became bogged down with the first. If I had known about slicing down, I would have organized my life to earn my PhD within three years; then I would have begun medical school. I would have worked backward, month by month, accomplishing what was needed in order to accomplish even bigger goals.

You can use the concept of slicing to achieve more abstract goals too. While generosity sounds like something rather intangible, a developer named William Lyon made it tangible enough to touch, in the form of the Orangewood Children's Home, a refuge for molested and abused children in Orange County, California. In fact, Lyon gave more than $250,000 a year to this charity.

Though he may not have thought of it this way, Lyon took his principle of generosity and sliced it down to the tangible goal of giving a specific amount of money away. He then sliced his goal down again into the very specific action of giving money to a single charity, the Orangewood Children's Foundation.

Let's suppose a big, audacious goal for you is to work in the beauty industry. If you were to slice that down, it might be parsed into a smaller goal of becoming a beautician. You might slice it down further into enrolling in a two-year cosmetology program, in which you'd learn how to design hair and discover various other beauty secrets.

I recall years ago that I wanted to become famous. When I was fourteen, I went with a friend to a Herb Alpert concert at the San Diego Sports Arena. In the late 1960s, Alpert's group, the Tijuana Brass, was among the most popular in the nation. When I stepped into the arena, I was shocked to see at least ten thousand fans packed in the seats. As I sat there, I became obsessed with the thought of one day being someone special. I never again wanted to be just an unrecognized face in the crowd. I wanted to walk into a huge group of people and have everyone recognize me.

It's interesting. Many years later, I have engaged in writing books and speaking around the world. It's likely the outcome of what happened at that sports arena. Your beliefs and values stay with you. They become part of your unconscious, directing much of what you do every day.

This makes sense. Think about all the goals you once wanted to accomplish, but didn't have the mindset that you could achieve them. Often the reason you quit was that your goals didn't align with your beliefs and values. They weren't important enough for you, because you didn't believe in them enough.

I remember years ago being pushed to play basketball because of my height. I wanted to make the team but didn't have the motivation to practice as hard as some of the other kids. Predictably, I was cut. Even though I said otherwise, making the team wasn't valuable enough for me to make the sacrifices necessary in order to be a good player. I didn't have a Results-Focused Mindset. When I was cut, I took it personally as an affront to my ability and blamed the coach for not liking me.

Part of developing a Results-Focused Mindset is aligning what you want with what you are willing to work for. It's easy to fail attempting things you never wanted to do in the first place. That in turn leads to discouragement, and is an enemy of maintaining an effective mindset. Likewise, it's tough to discipline yourself to achieve better grades in college if you've never had a desire to get a college degree. It's equally tough to lose weight, no matter how many diet books you read, if a slim figure isn't really worth the effort to you. And no matter how many times you tell others that you really want to spend more time with your family, if you don't place sufficient value on doing so, you won't organize your work life to be home more.

It's very hard to achieve goals that are in direct contrast with your values. Goals are important, but values are their bedrock foundation. If the values and beliefs underlying your mindset are shaky, your goals will be as well.

According to a recent poll, 52 percent of executives said if they'd known early in their careers that they'd still be in their current jobs, they'd never have started that career in the first place. According to one study, 83 percent of us don't like our jobs and would quit for a better opportunity.

THE FOUR KEY COMPONENTS OF SETTING GOALS

Are you ready to set achievable goals? There are four key points to remember. They are:

1. Be specific. Think of tangible and specific goals you can work toward, such as "I want to complete my college education in five years" or "I want to be a top-level manager in my current company in five years." A desire to be successful is a common goal, but suc-

cess is different for everyone. You need to think about what's most important to you. Then slice the goal down into bite-sized pieces. Find specific words and phrases to describe it.

Likewise, use measurable criteria so that you can judge whether or not you've reached your goals. Don't worry if your goals seem big. There are no unrealistic goals, only unrealistic time frames. It may sound clichéd, but it's better to plan something big and fall short than to set your sights too low.

2. Schedule for short- (in the near future), medium- (in the next three to five years), and long-term (more than five years away) goals. Develop a long-term plan. Then set medium- and short-term goals to get there. When I consulted in the early 1980s with the New York Life Insurance Company, I asked a salesman for one goal that would motivate him. He said, "To be happy." I told him to write down three specific achievements that would contribute to his sense of happiness. He came up with a 560SEL Mercedes and $100,000 in liquid investments. He also wanted to be home at 5 p.m. daily so he could play with his kids.

3. Be willing to do what it takes to achieve your objectives. If your goal is to read a book each week, you're going to have to make the time to do it. This might mean watching less TV, taking public transportation, or sleeping less at night. Can you do this? Are you willing to do this?

My brother Kevin markets sales and staff training videos to small and medium-sized businesses. He is a brilliant leader, often coaxing stellar performance out of mediocre people. One salesperson, Robert, was on his way to making more money than he had ever dreamed of. The problem was that Robert would go out on drinking and drug binges for days at a time. Kevin gave him warnings that he ignored, and finally fired him. For two weeks, Robert begged for his job back. Kevin felt sorry for the young guy and hired him again. But he also let Robert know that if this behavior occurred again, he would be gone.

Within one month, Robert was again engaged in drinking and drugs. He didn't come to work for three days. Kevin asked him why he was willing to give up a job he said he so desperately wanted. Robert admitted that he didn't have the mindset to say no to his friends. This is another example of a fixed mindset. His friends were all he had. He didn't have the mindset to be able to get better, more mentally stable friends who would help him achieve his goals. Without a Results-Focused Mindset, he couldn't stay sober in the long term. Robert wasn't willing to risk rejection from his friends now for a greater pleasure later. Because of his poor mindset, he was vulnerable to the influence of bad friends.

4. Maintain a Results-Focused Mindset in your quest to achieve what you want. As Henry Ford said, "Obstacles are those frightful things you see when you take your eyes off your goal." Without the confidence in your ability to put dreams together, you only have aspirations that never become reality. One way to maintain a supportive mindset is to carry representations of your goals with you. For example, when I played pro tennis, one player confided to me that he carried a photo of the U.S. Open trophy in his wallet. Every morning he would take it out and stare at it during breakfast. It helped him stay motivated for the rest of the day.

You might set aside a few minutes every day to review pictures of your goals, to keep them constantly in mind. In this way you can take stock of your progress and make corrections to ensure that you're on target.

FOCUSING ON OUTCOMES

If a *goal* can be defined as an objective you wish to achieve by a certain date, an *outcome* is a goal you experience before you achieve it. Outcomes are goals you can actually see, hear, and feel. While owning a new house is a goal, seeing that house with vaulted ceilings, a cherry-wood kitchen, and a veranda overlooking the ocean is an outcome.

One of my mentors, Jeannie LaBorde, defined the difference between goals and outcomes this way: Goals and objectives are like a pencil box that has been newly opened. Outcomes, on the other hand, are the same pencils, sharpened and well used. Here is a five-step approach to creating outcomes:

1. Focus on a tangible outcome.
2. Be positive in how you plan for your outcomes.
3. Sense and perceive the way you will feel when you achieve your outcomes.
4. Make sure they fit neatly with the outcomes of those who are important to you. Use the outward -mindset concept here.
5. Make sure your outcomes incorporate short-, medium-, and long-term goals.

Let's look more closely at step one. For example, if your goal is to become rich, your outcome would be to specify the amount of money that will make you wealthy. More specifically, if the goal is to make a six-figure income, the desired outcome might be to make an annual salary of $101,500. You also need to visualize and experience what it will be like earn more than $100,000 in income.

If your goal is to have a better family life, your outcome might be to imagine yourself spending at least an hour per day with your spouse and kids.

If your goal is to become more educated, the outcome might be to achieve an MBA within three years. You would imagine what it would be like in the executive suite of a large company.

The second step in achieving outcomes is to be positive about the things you want. I heard one divorced parent say, "My goal is to make sure I keep my ex-husband from getting custody of my child." Did you recognize the "moving away from" meta-pattern? This isn't an ideal outcome, because this person may end up causing grief, not only for herself but for her child. A more positive outcome would be, "My goal is to make sure my child has a consistent and stable home life." Setting positive outcomes are easier to achieve, and prevent conflict with other aspects of your life.

Another kind of positive outcome occurs when you work toward something other people believe in. Take smoking as an example. Not only will other people be able to relate to your goal of quitting, they can encourage and help you stay motivated as you work toward your goal.

The third step is to perceive how you will feel when you have achieved your outcomes. As we've already seen, well-known researchers in language, neuroprocessing, and psycholinguistics have discovered that people primarily think using one of three senses: sight, sound, and feeling. It's easy to apply this information to step three.

For example, if your goal is to be wealthy and your desired outcome is to make $100,000 next year, you might visualize $100,000 in neat new green dollar bills, in a paper bag stamped by the U.S. Treasury. Or, as you flip your fingers through these bills, you might hear the sound cards make, as you shuffle them in a deck. Or you might imagine the slightly rough edges on these bills and note that the paper feels a bit more porous than the kind of writing paper you find in your notebook. In this way, you're able to see, hear, or feel your desired outcome before you actually achieve it.

You can't do this with goals. Goals are simply things you'd like to accomplish, while outcomes give you a way to actually experience the goal before you strive to achieve it.

The fourth step in achieving outcomes is to make sure your desires dovetail with the values of others in your life. I recently met a woman who wanted to spend money fixing up her house. Her husband's goal was to move into a new house. He didn't want to spend any more money on their existing home, so his wife's refurbishing goal was in direct conflict with his. If she had asked her husband more about his own desired outcomes, she might have discovered that he was interested in increasing the value of their home for later resale. If she had sold the refurbishing idea as a way to build resale value, they both might have been able to dovetail each of their outcomes together.

The fifth step in achieving outcomes is to create short-, medium-, and long-term goals and objectives. Let's use smoking again as an example. Suppose you want to stop smoking in three months. You might schedule a checkpoint for next week at which you'll be smoking three fewer cigarettes per day. You might also set a goal of how many cigarettes you will be smoking at the end of the three months.

Sculptor Auguste Rodin, when asked how he managed to create his remarkable statues, responded, "I choose a block of marble and chop off whatever I don't need." This might be a good approach when choosing outcomes. Whatever you do, don't copy the techniques used by the various law-enforcement agencies in this story.

The LAPD, the FBI, and the CIA were all trying to prove that they were the best at apprehending criminals. The president of the United States decided to give them a test. He released a rabbit into a forest, and each organization was assigned to catch it.

The CIA went in. They placed animal informants throughout the forest. They questioned all plant and mineral witnesses. After three months of extensive investigations, they concluded that rabbits did not exist.

The FBI went in. After two weeks with no leads, they burned the forest, killing everything in it, including the rabbit, and they made no apologies. The rabbit had it coming.

The LAPD went in. They came out two hours later with a badly beaten bear. The bear was yelling, "OK! OK! I'm a rabbit! I'm a rabbit!"

A couple of years ago I met a stressed mom who complained about all the work she had to do and the lack of time to do it in. She knew what she didn't want out of life but couldn't seem to think of what she *did* want. I asked her what she valued most, and of course she said her kids. I asked what her goals were for them, and she had a list of things she wanted for them: to have a good education, to be happy at home, to feel protected, and to feel loved all the time.

I asked her to tell me how she would know if her kids were getting a good education. She said they would be on the honor roll at school. I then asked her how she could ensure they made the honor roll. She said if they diligently completed their homework every day, they would make it.

Puzzled, I asked her how that would help her feel less stressed. She said that most of her stress came from the kids after school. They fought and messed the house up while she was making dinner. I asked, "If they did their homework every day before watching TV, kept out of your way while you were making dinner, and didn't fight, would you feel less stressed?"

She smiled and said, "If you can do that, I'll be your friend for life."

I went one step further. I asked her to think about what her dream house would look and sound like at the end of the work-day. She said, "It's all quiet. My kids are studying in their rooms. They pop in once in a while to ask me a homework question and say 'Thanks, Mom,' and go back to their work. I hear them talking to each other without bickering. I then ask them to come to dinner, and they both tell me their homework is done." The woman was surprisingly detailed in her mental picture of what a blissful household looked, sounded, and felt like.

Uncovering this overworked mom's values and goals was the first step towards creating the outcomes she wanted in her life. While a lot of work remained, she was now on the right track to do it—and in fact did do it.

Like this woman, you too can assess your values, set goals, and concentrate on outcomes to achieve the mindset necessary to make them come to life. This may be the stuff dreams are made of, but dreams can—with a Results-Focused Mindset—come true.

7

Using Behavioral Contracts

I know a man who gave up smoking, drinking, sex, and rich food. He was healthy right up to the point when he killed himself. —Johnny Carson

Mark and Julie have a marriage that really works—for them. They have three small children. Julie, by choice, is a stay-at-home mom. Since she's already at home and Mark typically doesn't arrive until shortly before six o'clock, Julie nearly always cooks dinner. She also cleans the kitchen afterwards while Mark plays with the kids and gets them ready for bed.

Though Julie is eminently capable of heading out to the garage, sorting the recyclables, and loading them into the minivan each week, that's a job Mark usually performs. He also fills the bird feeders, fixes and glues broken toys, and makes sure Julie has wood each morning to feed the wood stove during the winter months. He also sweeps up after bringing in each load of wood.

Julie does nearly all the cleaning. Mark will haul the heavy pail full of dirty diapers out to the laundry room for her if she asks, and he'll shake out the heavier rugs as well when needed. But she does all the vacuuming, dusting, and scrubbing of floors, walls, sinks, and toilets.

A carpenter friend of theirs, staying briefly with them during a home-improvement project he was helping with, commented to Julie one day that she "sure made things easy for Mark."

Julie was surprised. She responded, "He does a lot of things for me, too." The rewards of their system were tangible for Julie: Mark thoroughly appreciated her efforts in their home, and Julie was relieved she didn't have to spend time working in the garage or fixing toys or tightening up the insulation in their drafty old farmhouse—areas she was less interested in and, in some cases, less proficient at.

The rewards for Mark were tangible, too: Though he was capable of cooking and cleaning, he was glad he didn't have to worry about doing it. His interests lay elsewhere, and he was able to devote his spare time to them and still come home to a clean, pleasant house and hot meals on the table every night.

Somehow, without ever really discussing it, they'd come up with an arrangement that worked for both. They were both conscientious about holding up their ends of the bargain.

Branch Rickey, former owner of the Brooklyn Dodgers baseball team, once said, "Luck is the residue of design." Designing this luck can begin with contracts. Though Julie and Mark in the story above might not have thought about it in these terms, they were using a subtle form of a contract to keep their home—and their satisfaction with one another—in top shape.

Contracts are nothing new to most of us. We're all operating under one sort of contract or another, written or verbal. It might be a contract to work each day for our employer. It might be an unspoken contract with our neighbors to keep our yards clean. It might be the understanding we have with our partners to be considerate and kind even when we're having a bad day.

Though most of us have an Achilles' heel of one kind or another that makes it difficult for us to maintain a consistently effective mindset, society's laws—another word for contracts—teach most of us to take responsibility for at least our social actions.

Using a behavioral contract can help you change from a fixed, inward mindset to a Results-Focused Mindset. You'll also discover ways to reward yourself for activities or behaviors you want to develop, behaviors that in turn will help you achieve outcomes and stay in control of your life.

If you successfully complete the following four- to six-week behavioral contract, you'll find that commitment to your goals, as well as your overall enjoyment and achievement in life, will sky-rocket. It shouldn't take longer than this, because by the end of four to six weeks your new behavior should be habitual.

A behavioral contract is really a promise or agreement you make to yourself to help you develop into the person you want to be (though ideally you'll involve another person as your partner to help you increase your overall performance).

In turn, since it is well established that rewards are the most effective way to develop new habits or modify old ones, you'll reward yourself for keeping this promise or agreement. Most people use punishment as a motivation to change. While punishment can be effective in killing habits, it also causes resentment and ill feelings. Plain and simple, it's not as effective as rewards.

REWARDING YOURSELF

The value of rewards shows up early in our lives, first in small things. For instance, as a child, your parents might have thanked you for making your bed or picking up your toys. They may have expressed pride in your grammar-school achievements or showed up at your athletic events. Perhaps they set up regular play times for you, provided your homework was done by a certain time.

BEHAVIOR SHAPING

Your parents probably didn't think of it, but using rewards effectively is called *behavior shaping*. It works to mold and develop children, and it can work to create self-discipline for you. There are four ways to shape your own behavior.

1. Apply a reward to a specific behavior
2. Withhold a reward linked to a certain behavior
3. Apply punishment to a behavior
4. Consistently use the process of rewards to maintain a behavior

Let's look at them in more detail.

1. **Apply a reward.** Let's say you're trying to avoid eating between meals. It's hard to be a dieter, because food itself is rewarding. You have a lot of trouble resisting, so you make a deal. If you stop snacking for a week, you'll reward yourself with a new dress or sports coat.

2. **Withhold the reward.** Withholding the reward can work along the same lines. For example, you know the bills have to be paid by the first of the month, but you are always late in paying them. Your

utilities have even been shut off in the past because of your procrastination. It's not that you don't have the money; it's that you don't have the discipline to sit down and do your banking on time. So you make a deal with yourself that if you don't pay bills on a regular schedule throughout the month, you won't get to watch a TV show you really enjoy. (Of course, if you don't pay the bills and your electricity gets turned off, you won't be able to watch TV anyway.)

3. **Apply punishment.** Applying punishment is the third way to shape behavior, despite its obvious drawbacks. Suppose you need to study for a class an hour each night, but you never get to it. You might punish yourself by doing an hour of yard work for every hour of belated studying. It's sort of a double whammy, but again it's not the most effective way to develop a better mindset. For one thing, if you don't have a Results-Focused Mindset to study, you probably don't have the motivation to punish yourself for not doing it either.

4. **Consistently use the process of rewards.** This is the most effective way to develop a better mindset. Having a good mindset one time isn't enough to make it a habit. You must be consistent for several weeks to successfully shape a behavior.

With that said, the more quickly you receive a reward, the greater the impact it will have on your behavior. Think about the games you play at carnivals or county fairs. You spend a dollar at a game and have a chance of walking away with a prize. How likely would you be to spend that dollar if you had to wait for your prize to be mailed? Not very.

We do work for deferred rewards, of course, such as waiting for an investment to pay off, but deferred rewards have the least impact on our behavior. This also means they have the least ability to create a Results-Focused Mindset.

To be most effective, you need to use deferred rewards in conjunction with the behaviors you want to modify. Deferred rewards could come in the form of a bonus at the end of a year, or a wall plaque recognizing your work, or perhaps dinner out at the end of the week with your spouse, but you should give them to yourself only after you've reached certain goals for the week.

PICKING YOUR REWARDS

A behavioral contract that uses rewards will allow you to develop the self-discipline you need to achieve your goals. This means, first, that you need to determine which rewards hold the most pleasure and thus will be the most motivating for you. To do this, look at the worksheet labeled "Rewards and Reinforcers." Listed on it are some of the things you might feel are treats or rewards for self-disciplined actions. Take a moment now and check the ones that appeal to you the most. Also fill in the blank spaces on the bottom with any rewards you'd like to add to this list.

Next, go to the column labeled "Importance." On a scale of one to ten, rate the importance of each reward to you with one being the least important, and ten the most important. This rating is critical in effectively using rewards that work; only those activities you rate five or above are useful in creating self-discipline.

The next column is "Time Spent." This refers to the amount of time you spend doing an activity that you consider rewarding. Measuring the time you spend on an activity is important, because it has a bearing on whether you'll use it as an immediate or deferred reward. Obviously, you wouldn't take a trip every weekend to reward yourself for doing something that week, but you might take a long walk as an immediate reward for completing an activity.

REWARDS AND REINFORCERS

✓	Activities	Importance	Time Spent	Frequency
	Watching Television			
	Listening to the Radio			
	Cup of Coffee or Tea			
	Being alone			
	Reading a Newspaper			
	Reading a Book			
	Reading a Magazine			
	Exercise (Jogging, Spa, aerobics)			
	Hobby			
	Long Baths or Bubble Baths			
	Eating Favorite Foods			
	Going to a Movie, Play, Concert			
	Sports (Tennis, Skiing, Swimming)			
	Going out for dinner			
	Smoking			

The last column is "Frequency." How often do you engage in an activity you consider to be rewarding? Again, this has a bearing on whether you'll consider it a deferred or an immediate reward. It will also help you decide which reward will be the most effective in reinforcing desired behavior.

Now look at the worksheet called "Behavioral Contracts."

At the top of this sheet are two columns labeled "If" and "Then." The "If" column represents the target behaviors you want to be more self-disciplined about. Fill in the "If" section with statements such as, "If I make six cold calls each day," or "If I book one appointment per day," or "If I read one chapter each day," or "If I stay on my diet each day," or whatever it is that you want to be more self-disciplined about.

When you've done this, go to the "Then" column. "Then" statements stand for the reward you'll get from fulfilling the "If" statement and changing your behavior. After an "If" statement such as "If I make five sales phone calls each day," you might write, "Then I can watch the evening news."

The "Then" part of the contract can (but needn't) be drawn from the Rewards and Reinforcers sheet. Any reward can be used if you've rated it at an enjoyment or importance level of at least six.

Directly beneath the "If" and "Then" columns is a section labeled "Bonus." The bonus is a reward for successfully accomplishing the weekly goals and activities you've set for yourself. This bonus could be something like having dinner at a nice restaurant on Saturday evening after completing a week's goals. Essentially, it's anything you think would be rewarding and would reinforce your goals in the future.

Directly below the "Bonus" section is the "Control" section. For this you'll need a partner. Choose somebody, ideally your spouse or someone you work with, who can help you enforce this contract and

BEHAVIORAL CONTRACT

EFFECTIVE DATES: From _____ To _____

IF _____   THEN _____
_____   _____
_____   _____
_____   _____

IF _____   THEN _____
_____   _____
_____   _____
_____   _____

IF _____   THEN _____
_____   _____
_____   _____
_____   _____

BONUS: _____
_____
_____
_____

CONTROL: _____
_____
_____
_____
_____

_____
Goal Achiever

_____
Partner

This contract will be reviewed on _____
date

encourage you throughout the program. Since we humans often rationalize giving ourselves a reward even when we haven't earned it, a partner isn't just a good idea, but a necessary part of the plan to help keep you on track. Thus this partner needs to be someone you see daily, someone who's truly supportive of you, someone who can discuss your goals and accomplishments with you, and someone who can commit to supporting your efforts for the next four to six weeks—essentially, someone who understands your goals and desires and wants them for you almost as much as you want them for yourself.

Don't set yourself up for disappointment by using a possible competitor as a partner. There is a chance that if you select an office mate, they may see you as a competitor for a job they also want. If you suddenly improve your performance, for example, you may be that much closer to being selected for the position they also want.

When you approach your partner, you might suggest a two-way arrangement. If at some point your partner decides such a program might be a good idea for them, you'd agree to be their partner.

You need to interact with your partner about your progress on the program at least once a day. In addition, you need to complete a Weekly Activity Log that will enable your partner to see how much you've been doing. Set this log up by listing the days of the week, Sunday through Saturday, and next to each day recording the activity you engaged in that moved you closer to your goal.

You should also be prepared to do one more thing. To further help keep you committed to this program, write a check to your partner for $200 or more. If you fall short of your contractual obligations, if you fail to reward yourself when you've earned it, if you fail to interact with your partner, if you do not complete the weekly activities sheet, or if you decide to quit the program for any reason except because you've changed your goals, you forfeit the $200 to your partner. If you quit before the four- to six-week period is up, your partner must cash the check with or without your permission and spend it any way he or she sees fit.

Now select a goal you wish to start working toward during the next four to six weeks. If it's a major goal, like making $100,000 a year, slice it down by dividing by twelve. This will tell you the amount you need to make each month: around $8500. If you break it down further, you'll need to make about $2000 a week. You could even break that down to a daily target if you like.

Your Results-Focused Mindset produces your behavior. The reason we have spent so much time on goals and outcomes is that with a great mindset, achieving goals become easier and less stressful. So creating a reward-based approach to hitting your goals also has an impact on creating a better mindset. It can strengthen the belief that you can hit any goal you want and overcome any obstacle in the future.

A computer-accessory salesperson I worked with was never able to hit his goals. He always seemed to get distracted by obstacles. With each failure, his mindset suffered, as he lost any confidence that he could actually improve his life. When you set goals without hitting them, you don't set any more goals. He wanted to own a Pearson thirty-one-foot yacht, which cost approximately $50,000. The salesman earned only about $2000 a month. He made about two sales a week, eight sales a month, and his average commission was approximately $250. You can see that it would be difficult at best to buy the yacht outright or even lease one. He also set a goal to purchase that yacht within two months. Because his goal depended on a larger income, he needed to increase his sales. His averages dictated that to get one sale, he had to see about two prospects. To see two prospects, he had to book about three appointments. To book three appointments, he needed to call ten referrals.

His average activity showed that he was calling approximately twenty people a week. He was booking about two appointments a day and seeing about two prospects a day, which yielded him two sales per week, for a weekly grand total of $500. The lease on the yacht would cost him around $600 a month. For this salesperson, that meant generating about three more sales per month. This translated into calling thirty more referrals per month, or about eight more referrals a week. He also would have to book nine more appointments and see six more prospects per month. This would have to be done over and beyond the number of sales he needed to maintain his current standard of living.

If this seems like a lot of work, keep in mind the law of *forced efficiency*. This holds that if you push yourself to do something, you'll always find an easier way to do it. In this particular example, the salesperson, when faced with making more calls, found easier and better ways to hit his goals. Eventually he wasn't doing that much more work. He was just improving his efficiency, and, as a result, his productivity and income. He wasn't working harder; he was working smarter.

The way this individual started on his program was very simple. We knew how hard he was working in terms of activity—he was making around four referral calls per day, booking about two appointments per day, and seeing around two prospects a day. He was also making a sale on average every two days. Although he'd ultimately have to increase his activity, we started him at his current normal activity level to get him adjusted to the program.

His Rewards and Reinforcers sheet indicated that, on an importance level of six or more, he enjoyed watching television, playing tennis, and drinking coffee. He also enjoyed going out to dinner on the weekends. We decided to link the coffee drinking to phone calls.

For every call he made, he could take a sip of his coffee. If he made no phone calls, he didn't get coffee that day. Since he also liked to watch television in the evening, we linked television time (about an hour each evening) to appointments. If he went on an appointment, he could watch TV that evening. If there were no appointments that day, there was no television either.

If this seems harsh, don't believe it. It was all his idea. These were rewards he was already getting. On his new program, they became reinforcers that he could now use to stay committed to his goals.

The last reward linked to an activity was tennis. Since this guy really enjoyed playing tennis for a couple of times a week, we linked seeing prospects to playing tennis. For every two prospects he saw, he would receive an afternoon or evening of playing tennis. There was no reward given for the number of sales he made. If his activities increased, we knew sales would follow. The bonus for the salesman was that if he accomplished all his goals for the week, he could go out to a nice restaurant as a reward.

During this individual's second week, he increased his phone calls by one per day. It wasn't until the fourth week that he also increased his booked appointments, as well as the number of prospects he saw during the day. By making a slow, steady increase, he was able to adjust to the extra activity while preventing stress and strain. He also adjusted to rewarding himself or not giving himself rewards, depending on whether fulfilled the activity required. He was slowly but surely developing self-discipline. By the sixth week, he tripled the number of sales he was making because he had tripled his sales activity. Later, it didn't take him long to maintain the higher level of sales, even though he was working less. He just learned to work smarter and better. He bought his yacht for cash without even having to get a loan or a lease.

In another case, I worked with a manager who didn't seem to have the time to read more business-related articles and books. His target behavior was to develop a Results-Focused Mindset that he could increase his income by increasing his job efficiency. When you improve your skill set, you make more money. His goal was to read one chapter per day, which he kept track of on his Weekly Activity Log. He saw numerous benefits to his goal. By reading, he would get more information that would make him more valuable to his company. He would also be in a good position to directly increase his pay, because of the new skills he would pick up through the reading. He would also develop more interest in his job, because he would know more about the industry in general.

We started this manager off by putting him on a very simple program in which we encouraged him to read one more page per day. It usually took him only a minute or so to do this, but just getting the book out, looking at the page, and reading it was enough to start a habit of reading. In time, we increased the number of pages he read. Most important at first was just getting a book in front of him.

We found from his Rewards and Reinforcers sheet that he enjoyed walking around the block at noon. On his importance scale, walking was an eight. So every time he read one page at lunch, he could have his noon walk. After the fourth week, his goal was increased. He was rewarded with a walk only after reading five pages. His activity was slow, and it took about six weeks before he was actually reading ten pages, or a chapter, per day. Once he met his reading goals on each of the five workdays, his bonus was playing eighteen holes of golf on the weekend.

Another salesperson I worked with, at a major stock-brokerage company, hated prospecting. In fact, he flatly didn't do it, and his business was at the point of failing. Even in the face of failure, he still couldn't force himself to make cold calls or calls to referrals. I asked him what he liked to snack on in the morning. He told me bananas. So I linked the reward of one small piece of banana to every phone call he made. About a month later, after using the banana as a reward, he reported that his cold calls and referral calls had increased 150 percent! He thought it was silly, but every time he made a cold call, he'd give himself a small piece of banana. Even though it seemed childish, he still was able to associate a pleasurable experience, the fruit snack, with a nonpleasurable experience, the phone call. Getting on the phone became much more enjoyable.

Frequently people using this method say to me, "Kerry, I'm smoking two packs of cigarettes a day, but my objective is to stop smoking, and I want to stop tomorrow. How can I develop a new mindset to accomplish this?" The truth is you need to have a systematic program by which you can change gradually and permanently. Without such a program, most people will never sustain the change.

Also, while I encourage you to increase your activity after your first week or so of using reinforcers, or as soon as you feel comfortable, always start at your present level of activity. Stay at that level for a week or two until you adapt. If you make too many changes, you will get stressed and quit. Only after you have adapted should you increase your activity. Don't move on to the next level until you've grown accustomed to the current level.

For example, one salesperson making only a few phone calls to get business began making one hundred calls per day. By the third day, he found he couldn't keep up the pace and failed to hit his goals.

By the same token, I can't stress enough how important it is to immediately take a reward when you've earned one. Immediate rewards help you increase activity much faster. Many individuals I have worked with give themselves a sip of fruit juice or maybe a couple of nuts for every phone call they make.

REWARD TOKENS

Another way to use an immediate reward to increase your activity or target behavior is by using tokens. After all, most of us probably shouldn't eat a piece of candy after every phone call. Tokens work equally well to give you an immediate reward at times when you don't want or shouldn't have your usual reward. They can be such things as poker chips, pennies, or even paper clips.

For example, you can state on your behavioral contract that you will receive one token each time you say something nice to an employee, or one token every time you ask for a sales referral. I have a colleague, Bill Cates, who talks about developing a referral mindset. What he means by this is constantly remembering to ask for referrals. You can't eat a piece of candy every time you ask. But you can give yourself a token.

Each token might represent one half-hour of television time or a cup of coffee. For every five tokens, you might give yourself time to play tennis or even an hour of golf. For every ten tokens, you might receive time reading just for pleasure in the evening.

You might decide to use tokens as a means to get to work earlier so that you could develop a mindset of being on time. I really do think this is a mindset issue. But being late also communicates that your time is more valuable than the time of the person you are meeting.

At first, you could give yourself a token just for leaving your house ten minutes earlier in the morning. Later on in the week or month, you'd give yourself a token only if you arrive on time. Still later you'd give yourself a token only if you were early. This is a way of easing yourself into a new, on-time mindset.

A psychologist friend of mine used to work with the University of Michigan football team. The Wolverines are among the best NCAA football teams in history, but they weren't always so successful. Years ago my friend decided that tokens might be an effective tool to get Michigan's players to develop a winning mindset. Most coaches know that winning is actually a mindset. You can learn how to win or learn how to lose, but both are mindsets.

The coaching staff, on the advice of the psychologist, started putting little stickers on the player's helmets. For every big tackle they made or every fumble they recovered, they would get a sticker. The tight ends and the wide receivers received stickers for every catch they made.

To their surprise, the coaching staff found the players would do practically anything to get a sticker! They would jump over people, mow players down, practically go through brick walls to get one of those tokens. The Wolverines learned how to tackle harder, fumble less, and recover their fumbles more frequently. It's a lot like the Army giving stripes to denote rank, or medals to award valor. It's basically a symbol of what each of us works for: recognition through a reward that all can see and admire. This is often more valued than money, which, by the way, is itself just a kind of token.

By using a contract, one you've designed with rewards for behavior that contributes to hitting your goals, you'll be surprised at how quickly your behaviors change. What's more, you can use this contract to change or reinforce any behavior you want. All you have to do is stick with it. When you do, you're keeping one of the most important agreements you'll ever make—an agreement with yourself to develop a Results-Focused Mindset and hit your goals.

8

How Mindset Changes Your Brain

So far we have discussed how mindsets are critically important because they lead to better learning behavior, which in turn creates better learning outcomes. Some studies have shown a relationship between beliefs and brain activity. When someone with a Results-Focused Mindset makes a mistake, they experience more brain activity than those with a fixed mindset. The brains of people who believed in their ability to improve and overcome obstacles acted differently when a mistake was made than the brains of those who did not expect improvement.

In fact, those with a Results-Focused Mindset seemed to have a greater awareness of errors than those with a fixed mindset. The authors concluded that they were more likely to correct their mistakes. Those with a growth mindset experienced enhanced brain reaction and paid more attention to the mistakes in an attempt to improve.

In a fixed mindset, there is a sense that what you are now is all you will ever be. Therefore to establish value and self-worth, you must dismiss your setbacks and failures instead of working harder to correct them. A fixed mindset also produces negative thinking.

According to neuropsychologist Rick Hanson, people are naturally wired with a bias towards negative thinking. Our minds tend to discard the good news and focus on the bad. It's kind of like when someone says, "I have good news and bad news. Which do you want first?" The natural response is, "Give me the bad news. The good news is not as important." Hanson believes that we have evolved to think this way. If you are a caveman and avoided a threat, you'd have another opportunity later to collect food. But if you were unable to avoid the threat, the good news of available food would be irrelevant. Evolutionary psychologists believe that much of how we behave and how our brains are structured is primarily the result of evolution from a time when we first walked the earth barefoot with skins and clubs.

But brain structures do seem to have evolved. In a recent study of millennials, around 20 percent sought help or advice for workplace depression. This is a higher percentage than in any other generation before. Millennial women from eighteen to thirty-four years old reported 4.9 days of poor mental health per month, while millennial men had an average of 3.6 poor mental health days per month. Our brains are very focused on stress, even when it is unremarkable and non-life-threatening. But here's the interesting part. Negativity produces more brain activity than do equally positive events. For example, Hanson discovered that people can identify angry faces faster than happy ones. Most of the studies are done with a T-scope, in which faces are flashed for only a tenth of a second. A threat, created for example by an angry face, causes a flight or fight response. This means that someone will either stand and fight the threat or run away. The brain area responsible for this response is the limbic system.

So it seems as though your brain is coated with Velcro for negative experiences and Teflon for positive ones. One of the most difficult things to change in a mindset is to preserve the positive experiences longer in the memory and forget the negative experiences more quickly. Another brain structure, called the amygdala, is responsible for this thought pattern. You've got two of these almond-shaped regions, one on each side of your head, which are primed to pick up negativity. Once the amygdala is triggered, negative events and experiences are stored quickly in memory. In contrast, positive experiences need to be held in your memory for at least fifteen to thirty seconds to be transferred from the buffers of your short-term memory into long-term memory.

For years, I have said in seminars that in one day we forget 70 percent of what we hear in one day, and 90 percent within three days. This is because of the difficulty in transferring what we just learned five minutes ago into what we retain in three days. You can build up your long-term memory by repetition or by increasing your attention. For example, if I want to remember a telephone number, I can repeat it five times, wait a day, and repeat it five more times tomorrow. This spaced repetition is sure to help transfer the event into long-term memory. One way to remember a telephone number is to associate it with events in your life or experience. For example, if I wanted to remember 405-6297, I would associate it with the 405 freeway in Southern California, my age today, and what I think my life expectancy will be. It only takes thirty seconds to remember this and transfer it to long-term memory.

The reason I discuss how to remember things is that you can change your negative mindset into a positive one by paying more attention to the good things that happen to you than the negative ones. Because our brains are structured to focus on and remember negative things, you really need to work at focusing on and remembering the positive experiences. So by holding the positive events in mind for at least thirty seconds, and recalling them throughout your day, you're more likely to change to a more positive mindset. This will also actually change the physical structure and the makeup of your brain.

ARE YOU A RUMINATING WORRIER?

Some researchers discuss *rumination*: continually recalling a situation and focusing on its negative aspects. The more you focus on a negative event, the more you'll reinforce a negative mindset.

I was at a Christmas party recently and learned that an event planner at my tennis club was retiring. I mentioned this to a woman, and she said she was very happy. She instantly recalled a tennis tournament in which the event planner was rude. Then she recalled another episode in which the same event planner made a mistake. Finally she remembered two more interactions resulting in a bad ending. This one retirement announcement triggered a cascade of bad memories in the woman, with not one positive memory. I really wanted to tell her about the differences between the fixed and Results-Focused Mindsets, but I'm sure she would have just rolled her eyes at me. It was better to be empathetic than correcting. In any case, this is how a negative mindset occurs. Ruminating frequently on an unpleasant event only strengthens your memory of it.

According to an article in *Psychology Today* magazine, rumination can actually damage the neural structures of your brain that regulate emotions, memory, and feelings. Even when the worry and stress are not based on reality, the amygdala and the thalamus (another part of the brain, which helps communicate sensory and motor functions) are unable to differentiate worries from real threats.

One hormone that reacts to stress is cortisol. This hormone breaks down the hippocampus, the part of the brain that helps form new memories. Many of us may feel stress and anxiety in the morning, indicating high levels of cortisol, which tend to dissipate throughout the day.

One of my favorite movies is *Broadcast News*. In one of the first scenes, a female producer gets ready to go to work in the morning. She looks in the mirror, ready to go, and bursts into five minutes of a tearful meltdown. But the crazy thing is, she does this routine every day. She gets all the anxiety out in the morning, preparing the way for less stress at work. Nonetheless, the more cortisol that is released in response to negative experiences, worry, and rumination, the more difficult it can be to form new positive memories.

In neuroscience there is a concept called *experience-dependent neuroplasticity*. This means that when neurons fire together, they wire together. That is, our brains create physical structures reflecting our memories, whether they are positive or negative. This may be too much detail for you, but your experiences and thoughts create new synapses between your neurons, making it easier to remember those experiences. Your memories can actually change your genes and alter the structure of your brain. In other words, the brain is shaped by your mindset.

MINDFULNESS

You're probably scared enough now that you don't want to think at all. In a way, that's exactly what the experts want you to do. One technique in cognitive psychology is called *mindfulness*. This is a nonjudgmental awareness of moment-to-moment experiences. As you experience events with mindfulness, you move into a type of meditative state in which you do not characterize events as either good or bad.

Remember when your mother told you to count to ten before you got mad? She was probably right. The process of counting was to get you to detach your emotions from what had just happened and relax enough to make a better emotional decision.

Many years ago, one of my colleagues suggested putting a drop of fingernail polish on a watch. This was to remind you of your thoughts every time you checked your watch. For example, as you look at it and see the drop of red polish, you ask yourself if your thoughts are positive or negative. Now you know that the amount of time you spend in each memory will actually change the structure of your brain, causing those memories to be more easily recalled. Therefore, every time you look at the drop of fingernail polish and immediately substitute a memory of a recent positive experience for a negative thought, you are closer to eliminating the worry.

PATTERN INTERRUPT

My favorite technique to move from a negative mindset to a positive one is called *pattern interrupt*. Pattern interrupt will help you move from a fixed, inward mindset into a results-focused growth mindset. Irrational thoughts seem to feed on and compound themselves, like a snowball that increases in size as it rolls down a snowy hill. By recognizing when these patterns are setting in, you can interrupt the thoughts.

Next time you observe that worry has surfaced, immediately do something physical. Stand up and walk around your office. Say out loud what you are thinking.

One of the best ways to interrupt a negative thought pattern is to create quick physical discomfort. Wear a rubber band around your wrist, and when you slip into a negative mindset, snap the rubber band. The sting will break the pattern. You can, for example, use the drop of nail polish on your watch to remind yourself to check, then snap the rubber band if you see that your thoughts have turned negative.

SUBSTITUTION

You could also immediately substitute a positive experience replacing a negative one. For example, when you hit an obstacle and start to worry, snap the rubber band and remember how you were able to overcome a similar block in the past.

REWARD, RINSE, AND REPEAT

Finally, give yourself immediate rewards. A reward can be anything from a sip of coffee to calling your spouse—or even popping a breath mint into your mouth. The reward reinforces the action of the phone call and increases the likelihood that you will make another call.

A financial planner I once coached recently used this four-step technique. He had a fixed mindset telling him that he didn't have the talent to sell. He knew that contacting potential clients was the only way to grow his business, but he had call reluctance. His heart palpitated and sweat beaded on his forehead before each call. Then (1) he observed his own phobic reaction, (2) interrupted himself with a rubber-band snap, (3) substituted a memory of a successful call, and (4) drank a cup of coffee as a reward. Not only did his anxiety decrease, but he finally was able to grow his business.

9

How Struggle Can Create a Better Mindset

Expert Carol Dweck has written about how difficult it is to keep a healthy mindset when everything is falling apart. I've already discussed how your brain is wired to focus on negativity. As you fall prey to the temptation to think negatively, you will create deeper neural pathways along these line. The more you ruminate on negativity, the more the brain restructures itself to keep you negative.

In the new book *Rush,* author Todd Buchholz tells us that struggle and challenge are what help you create a Results-Focused Mindset. When you become ambitious and take on new challenges, the brain produces serotonin and dopamine. Dopamine is the euphoria drug of the brain. The more of it you produce, the better you will feel. There are dopamine receptors in the brain that act like the sound waves hitting your inner ear. As these receptors are triggered, you feel better. Dopamine receptors are one reason people overdose on drugs. Cocaine, heroin, and methamphetamine trigger these receptors. Unfortunately, they also diminish the receptors' ability to produce euphoria in time. The receptors actually decrease in size; it is much like getting a haircut. The user then has to take a greater quantity of drugs to get him high. But these drugs are so toxic that as the dose increases, the chance of death goes up as well.

When you take on a new project, neurons begin to make new connections. Gray cells process information for the central nervous system, allowing the brain to regenerate. Remember when you had a couple of alcoholic drinks and friends said that you'd just killed a couple of billion brain cells that will never grow back? Well, that was partly true and partly false. You *can* kill brain cells with alcohol. But research over the last decade has shown that brain cells actually do go back through cognitive engagement. This is learning, communicating, and challenging yourself. What *does* cause brain-cell death is inactivity. When we become less mentally and physically active, PET brain scans show that serotonin levels dip and gray cells start dying.

If you play hooky from work or become lazy, you can actually decrease your mental and physical life expectancy. Many of my friends say they want to keep working till they reach seventy, but that at the age of sixty-two, they want to reduce their work week to two days. But is it really healthy not to be challenged and engaged the other five days? Engagement in work, and the rewards it produces, are like an audience applause. Engaging in and completing a task releases serotonin and dopamine. That makes you feel good.

WHY YOU NEED TO STRUGGLE

Buchholz makes a direct assertion: if you want to go downhill really fast, retire today. Retirement creates a drop in your cognitive ability, even when adjusting for age and health issues. As people get close to retirement, they can't recall as many words or think as clearly as their age-group peers who keep struggling.

The research among retirees is striking. In the United States and Denmark, a man in his early sixties is 33 percent less likely to be working than a man in his fifties. In France and Austria, the number rises to 85 percent. Here's the shocking part. The cognitive ability of men in their sixties drops twice as much in Austria and France is in the United States and Denmark. The following story illustrates this beautifully.

A man once found the cocoon of a butterfly. He began keeping an eye on it and one day noticed that a small opening had appeared. The man sat and watched for several hours as the butterfly struggled to force its body through the little hole. Then the butterfly seemed to stop making any progress. It appeared as though it had gotten as far as it could and could go no further. The man decided to help the butterfly. He took a pair of scissors and snipped off the remaining bit of the cocoon. The butterfly then emerged easily, but it had a swollen body and small, shriveled wings.

The man continued to watch the butterfly, because he expected that, at any moment, the wings would enlarge and expand to be able to support the body, which would contract in time.

Neither happened. In fact, the butterfly spent the rest of its life crawling around with a swollen body and shriveled wings. It never was able to fly.

In his kindness and haste, the man did not understand that the restricting cocoon and the struggle required for the butterfly to get through the tiny opening were nature's way of forcing fluid from the body of the butterfly into its wings so that it would be ready for flight once it achieved its freedom.

Work engages and strengthens your brain as well as building neural circuits. Disengaging from work also disengages the same circuits. Is actual retirement or preparing for retirement the problem? When you start planning for retirement, whether at age fifty-five or sixty-five, your brain disengages and decreases your cognitive ability. Why challenge yourself and learn new tricks to succeed if you don't plan on using them? This is why it's so critical to consistently maintain a Results-Focused Mindset. The more we struggle to learn, the more mentally acute we become, and the longer we live. But what kind of work keeps you the most engaged? Buchholz says anything that puts food on the table. Pretty much anything that earns money.

A few years ago, I kept hearing of older friends telling me how wonderful retirement is. They see their kids more, they travel more, and they seem to be having a lot of fun. This looks like a pretty attractive option when normal business problems keep you up at night. Bren, one of my gym workout friends, has the opposite view. As a result of a corporate restructuring, a few years ago he was pushed out of his job as a midlevel manager at State Farm Insurance. At sixty-five, he had been hoping to work until he reached seventy at least. He very honestly said, "Retirement is OK, but I really wish I could've kept working. I really felt more relevant. I felt like I was making a contribution. I was making a difference. Retirement is fine, but life now is just not as interesting."

This is much the same comment I get from many other retirees, especially those who are leaving jobs they enjoyed. You *should* retire from a job you don't like. But because of the brain research showing how much cognitive ability atrophies from nonuse, you should find a job you *do* like. This is why retiring at sixty-five or seventy shouldn't actually mean retirement; it should mean transitioning. You should just do something else—something more challenging that also makes you an income.

But the really lucky people are those with a passion. These are the ones with a true Results-Focused Mindset. They're trying to save the world. They're always looking for a new idea or a new way to engage better. Medical researchers, who spend their whole lives searching out cures for cancer, hate retirement. They always feel that the next week or month could produce a breakthrough. Einstein died with a pen in his hand, writing out mathematical formulas explaining the universe. Edison didn't spend his last decade in a rocking chair overlooking his estate. He died from the complications of diabetes while he was still inventing and struggling.

So the key to staying engaged in your work is making sure it is also your passion. If you are passionate, keep doing it. You'll live longer and stay mentally sharper. If it's not your passion, find something that is, and stay engaged.

Buchholz discusses the case of hospital janitors. It's not a very glamorous position. They clean up after sick and dying people, who often can't control their bodily functions. Some hate the job, while others love it. What's the difference? Those who love being a janitor cherish the times they can touch a patient's hand, add water to their flowers, engage with visitors, and bring a smile to those who are ill in a hospital bed. These are the ones who feel a passion, a calling, a mission. Those who hate their jobs are just mopping floors.

So the Results-Focused Mindset isn't just willing to learn and stay positive yourself. People with this mindset keep themselves engaged. In turn they stay sharper and live longer. They are less bored and keep themselves much more mentally acute than those with a fixed mindset.

DEVELOPING A RESULTS-FOCUSED MINDSET IN YOUR BUSINESS

Perhaps one of the best applications of a great mindset is in business. Perhaps no other area of your life can it make a more dramatic difference than in your career. You can also influence and lead other people more effectively with a better mindset. Eighty-three percent of new businesses fail in the first three years. Coincidentally, 83 percent of American workers don't like what they do. This means that your attitude, how you influence the people you work with, and the mindset you use in your communication have a strong correlation to how much money you make.

I've been a business coach and speaker for more than thirty-five years. I've never met a single client in all that time who possesses a Results-Focused Mindset with goals who was not able to increase their business by at least 50 percent per year. In fact, most of my clients with those attributes increase their business by more than 80 percent per year.

I used to say to potential clients that I require three things before they start working with me:

1. They have to show up and be on time to our coaching appointments.
2. They have to study the things we talk about for at least five minutes every day.
3. They have to do the things they say they will do.

Every single coaching candidate I've spoken to over the last three decades has agreed to these stipulations. Often they say it will be easy. After hundreds of clients, only about 30 percent have actually kept their promises. The rest get distracted, lose focus on their goals, or just quit. They self-sabotage. They don't fail because of poor skills or the economy; they fail because of their fixed mindset. It's only those with a Results-Focused Mindset who see dramatic increases. Having an outward and growth-focused mindset makes all the difference.

Malcolm Gladwell, author of many best-selling books, refers to the perils of the wrong mindset. He claims that the talent mindset, which created the Enron culture, was also a major factor in the destruction of Enron as a company. Enron committed a fatal mistake by creating a culture that worshiped intelligence and talent at the expense of hard work. In other words, they created a culture with a fixed mindset. When Enron was confronted with bad decisions, they covered it up. In some cases, for example, Ken Lay and Jeff Skilling, executives actually lied and committed felonies. Instead of growing from their mistakes, they protected their fixed image.

Fixed-mindset people focus on justifying their talent and intelligence, while growth-mindset people constantly improve. In one study, Carol Dweck asked students to write a letter to someone in another school describing their results in a recent test. Forty percent of the students lied about their scores, but they always lied in an upward direction. Fixed-mindset people look for reasons to justify their talent. They also feel threatened when that image is questioned. They have a hard time taking remedial courses and admitting failure and setbacks, and refuse to take responsibility.

Fixed-mindset people also have a very difficult time admitting when they make mistakes. You've probably seen this in government. When a terrorist attack happens and there's not enough security, as in the attack on Benghazi, Libya, State Department officials blame others. They refuse to take responsibility. When IRS officials single out certain groups politically for special inspections, they deny even the most obvious pieces of evidence. When a city's murder rate spirals out of control, a mayor blames a lack of funding instead of his own mistakes. The first rule in becoming a good leader is first to admit mistakes, and then to learn and fix them. It's amazing to me how forgiving constituencies are when a political leader admits mistakes and announces plans to fix them. But usually they blame someone or something else. A powerful line we rarely hear is "I have made mistakes and am working on it. It's not where I want it to be right now, but we will make it happen."

According to Jim Collins in his book *Good to Great*, the best leaders are self-effacing. They are not larger-than-life, charismatic leaders with big egos. They are the leaders who are constantly able to confront challenges and ask questions. They confront hard choices with a Results-Focused Mindset of being able to overcome any obstacle. Great leaders don't try to prove how much better they are than anyone else, they just try to improve. Jack Welch, former CEO of General Electric, once said, "I am constantly trying to recruit people who are smarter than me."

Researchers Robert Wood and Albert Bandura, (Bandura is one of my graduate-school heroes) created an experiment that proved the value of a results-focused growth mindset and the destructiveness of a fixed one. They put graduate students into two groups, those with fixed and those with growth mindsets. They were to assign imaginary employees into the jobs appropriate for their stated skills. They then were told to decide how to best motivate and lead the workers. They also had to revise their management decisions based only on the feedback they received about employee productivity.

The fixed-mindset students were told that the task measured their own capabilities. The growth-mindset students were told their management skills were measured through practice, and the results of the task would give them an opportunity to improve their skills. Those students with a growth mindset kept learning. The fixed-mindset students worried about measurements of their performance or about protecting their fixed abilities. The growth-mindset people used their mistakes to learn how to accomplish their tasks better. Of course the fixed-mindset students also made mistakes in completing the tasks. But they gave excuses and assigned blame when they encountered setbacks instead of learning from them.

Lee Iacocca was an industry titan who was credited with turning around the Chrysler Corporation after bankruptcy. Jim Collins described Iacocca in a different way. Iacocca had with great talent and a huge ego. He was able to borrow money from the U.S. government and save hundreds of thousands of automotive jobs. He was successful in that one task. But his position was also one of talent worship. He didn't develop the lieutenants under him, focusing only on his own ability. As soon as he left Chrysler, it collapsed into mediocrity.

THE MINDSET OF GREAT LEADERS

When Jack Welch took over GE in 1980, the company had a $14 billion value. Twenty years later it was capitalized at $490 billion. It was the most valuable company in the world before Apple. GE was a conglomerate with many different businesses, but if there was a problem, Welch would often go directly to the factory floor and ask workers for their opinion and how they would fix it. Many of Welch's disciples learned from his experience and dramatically improved their leadership abilities. Welch never ran GE from an ivory tower. He realized he couldn't learn or improve unless he got the right information from the right sources. In short, he had a growth mindset. Lee Iacocca and the Enron executives, on the other hand, made decisions based on fixed mindsets.

I feel a personal connection to Jack Welch. I was a stockbroker in 1980 with investment banking firm, Kidder, Peabody and Company. Shortly after I left, GE bought Kidder. They did this because of hubris. At that time they thought any acquisition would make money because they were the smartest people in the room. But even though GE was populated by executives with a Results-Focused Mindset, Kidder, Peabody was not. Kidder went down the tubes when a bond trader, Joseph Jett, made fraudulent trades, claiming massive profits on each. Kidder, Peabody and Joseph Jett had fixed mindsets. If their results did not match up to their mindset, they would lie instead of learn.

I will be honest with you. That was the first and only job I was ever fired from. In was in 1981 in Newport Beach, California. I would make 150 cold calls every day, and get rejected on 149. The joke was: one call per day was to my mother, and after three months even she would say, "Never call me again." I once approached my manager, Steve, and asked if he would support me in speaking about investments to service groups and investment clubs around California. I had a lot of experience speaking in front of groups, and realized that most of my cold calls were to people who really didn't understand how investments worked. They didn't know about diversification or dollar-cost averaging, or even about how to allocate their retirement portfolios. After Steve heard my idea, he fired me on the spot. I remember his exact words. He said, "You aren't long for the business." This is stockbroker talk for "you will never make it." He then said that I needed to cold-call like everybody else, and he didn't see me being able to do that. My manager had a fixed mindset. There was only one way to sell, and that was his way—to cold-call.

Actually Steve did me a great favor. That same month I started my consulting practice, and after forty years, I've made far more money speaking and writing than I ever could have as a cold-call cowboy. But the experience of being on the telephone day after day did help me build my practice today.

Another of my heroes when I was growing up was Warren Bennis. A management professor at the University of Southern California, Bennis once said that many managers are driven and driving, but going nowhere. The best leaders, on the other hand, are inclusive and focused on praising effort, not talent. They don't praise employees by telling them how smart they are; instead they praise them by focusing on the great job they've done, or on their effort so far. Sure, it's about the task. But more importantly, praise is about the journey. One task well done is praiseworthy. But a career well executed is golden.

One of my favorite movies is *Schindler's List*, directed by Steven Spielberg. I'm sure you've seen it. It won an Academy Award in 1994. In one scene, a building at a concentration camp collapsed in front of its German architect. A female Jewish engineer suggested to the German project supervisor that the cement footings were to blame. She pointed at the exact spots in the building that needed to be shored up. Immediately an officer pulled out his Luger and shot the woman in the head. While this is an extreme example, this image stuck with me for decades as an illustration of what a fixed-mindset manager can do to a company's profits and morale.

Recently I was referred to a president of a medium-sized company. One of the brokers, also my coaching client, suggested that I call the president to help increase sales. He had never heard of me, so I did an elevator speech, letting him know the three things I do for my clients:

1. I put them on a weekly business plan to keep them consistently active.
2. I rebuild their basic skills so they don't have to work more hours.

3. I build advanced skills so that once we hit their goals, they can go to new heights.

The president of the company actually said, "We are already doing that. We don't need your help." We never talked about money; we never talked about commitment, only his goals. Since he had a fixed mindset, he wasn't interested in hearing any other solutions aside from the ones he already had. Unfortunately, his solutions weren't working.

NEGOTIATING A GREAT MINDSET

One of the most important skills you can develop in business is negotiation. One of my best friends, negotiation expert Roger Dawson, says, "It's not what you deserve, it's what you can negotiate." But are great negotiators born or developed? Can negotiation really be taught?

Twenty years ago I was in Washington, D.C., waiting for an American Airlines flight. The flight was two hours late to Los Angeles. I asked the United ticket agent if he would take my nonrefundable ticket on American and use it on the United nonstop. He smiled and gave me a boarding pass for first class. I said, "I didn't think that nonrefundable tickets could be transferred to another airline." The United ticket agent said, "They can't." Now this was a lot of years ago, but there are two great business lessons here. First, he was able to put me in an empty seat on United, hoping that I would become their frequent flyer instead of American's. But the better lesson is, if you don't ask, you will never know the answer. It's kind of like the man who prays to God begging to win the lottery. After three days of promising God to give half the winnings to charity, feed hungry children, and everything else he can imagine, a booming voice comes down from heaven saying, "At least would you please buy a ticket!"

In one study, researchers Laura J. Kray and Michael P. Haselhuhn monitored subjects engaged in negotiations. Half were assigned a fixed mindset and half a growth mindset. The groups were divided into pairs and were each given the role of a recruiter or a candidate. Each pair negotiated salary, vacation time, and benefits. The growth-mindset subjects did twice as well as the fixed-mindset subjects. Those who persevered through stalemates in the negotiation did much better than those who gave up. In other studies by the same researchers, the growth-mindset students in a negotiation class again did much better than those with a fixed mindset. The growth-mindset students believed they could improve their hard work. The fixed-mindset students thought negotiation was mostly about raw talent.

Donald Trump wrote *The Art of the Deal*, a best seller decades ago. My favorite story was his negotiation with Harold Helmsley, another developer in New York City. Helmsley approached Trump, trying to negotiate the purchase of one of his hotels. Trump said he didn't know what Helmsley was talking about. The hotel wasn't for sale. Helmsley insisted that it was and wanted Trump to make an offer. Trump shook his head and walked Helmsley to the elevator. When the elevator doors opened, Trump said, "I'm so sorry for this wasted trip. But if you did want to buy the hotel, how much would you pay?" Trump ended up selling the hotel for much more than he would have if he had been an eager seller. This is a good example of how effective good negotiators can be. As my friend Roger Dawson once said, "Negotiation is the fastest money you will earn in your life."

10

Your Mindset and Relationships

You have learned so far that a fixed mindset can destroy results and a Results-Focused Mindset can create results. But one question you should be asking is; can you help develop a better mindset in others, especially your kids? I've often thought about the connection between self-confidence and mindset. Encouraging a child merely to be self-confident can keep them from creating a Results-Focused Mindset.

Telling people how smart or talented they are leads to a fixed mindset. Praising them for their effort and achievement is much more helpful in developing a Results-Focused Mindset. Self-confidence is, then, a by-product of a Results-Focused Mindset.

HELPING YOUR KIDS DEVELOP A GREAT MINDSET

Developmental psychologist Haim Ginott worked for his whole life with children. His recommendation agrees with what we've already seen: praise should not be directed towards the child's attributes, but toward their efforts and accomplishment. Today's politically correct culture recommends giving awards for participation instead of achievement, and therefore telling kids they're all winners instead of a few winners and a lot of losers. But if every child can win, why put in more preparation and effort? If there is no chance of being a loser, why try as hard?

Equally negative is calling your child (or yourself) bad at something. When you say to your child, "You are just not very good at math," you are reinforcing their lack of talent instead of pointing out a lack of effort. It's almost like to saying that your child is a born loser. A good parent would never say that. What if the child believes it? They would stop trying and slip into a life of failure. But calling your child gifted or talented can be just as bad. If your child believes that, they may stop trying thinking their gifts will consistently make them successful.

In one study, Carol Dweck taught students a lesson that included math history and stories about great mathematicians. For half the students, mathematicians were described as geniuses who easily created theories and discoveries. This sent the message to the students that some people are born smart and math comes easily to them. The other students were told that the mathematicians were passionate about math but had to work hard to make great discoveries. This approach conveyed a Results-Focused Mindset, in which hard work and a passion for math could create success in anyone.

Instead we praise kids for their talent, or for anything but effort. We say, "Great job. You did that project perfectly." Or we say, "You are so smart. You are amazing. "It's important to communicate that its effort that's important rather than ability. Praise hard work and commitment instead of talent.

So when your child is worried about a test or a project that is due, don't reassure them by saying how smart they are or that they can't fail. Instead, reassure them of how hard they worked, and tell them that no matter what their grade, it will improve next time.

I've made this mistake with my own kids. Many years ago, when I taught my daughter Caroline to throw a ball, I said she was a gifted athlete. She threw straight ahead and followed through perfectly. What I should have said was, "Great job. You are really getting this. You improved even more than the last time we played catch." Years later she started playing tennis and easily made the high-school JV team. But when she tried out for the varsity squad, I made the mistake of trying to encourage her by saying, "You're the best player on the JV team; you will easily make the varsity team." She did make the varsity squad. But if she had not, she would have thought of it as a personal failure instead of as a stepping-stone to work hard for the next tryout.

Here are common praising mistakes parents make their kids:

1. Telling your kid you think she's the best.
2. Telling your child she was better than the kid who won.
3. Telling her the sport or activity wasn't really important.
4. Saying that with her talent and ability, she is sure to win next time.

But the worst thing a parent can say is that the child didn't have the ability or talent to win.

My wife, Merita, often berates herself. Recently she was given a prescription by her doctor. I asked what it was. She said, "You know I have a terrible memory; why would you ask me that?" Sometimes she will bump into a chair or a table and say, "I'm so clumsy, I can't believe I ran into that chair." You may be thinking that this is just humility, but it also communicates a fixed mindset. It sends a message that suggests her memory will never improve, and she will never become more graceful. You may also engage in this kind of self-talk.

Do you play golf and say, "I'm a horrible player; I will never get better"? Have you ever seen anybody throw their golf clubs after a bad shot? I have. This merely shows a fixed mindset, communicating that the player will never improve, will never get better.

Sometimes after making a bad tennis shot, I will say, "That was so stupid. I can't believe I hit that." Roger Federer, the best tennis player in history, seems ice-cold, emotionless in competition. But as a junior he was known for temper tantrums, throwing his tennis racquet across the court after bad shots. His parents, like mine, refused to buy him a new tennis racket when he broke his own. It doesn't take long to learn to control your behavior when you have to spend $200 after a tantrum.

Many tennis parents constantly tell the kids how good they are instead of praising them for how hard they work. As we've seen with John McEnroe, praising people's ability only leads to frustration, blame, and anger when they don't win. What we want to do is praise them for hard work and commitment.

I coached my daughter Caroline's high-school JV tennis team. Often I would tell the girls how to hit a better volley or get more power on their serves. I'd played on the pro tennis tour for two years in the 1970s. Yet I would actually get some girls who would argue that what I was teaching wasn't the way their parents taught them. Or their would parents tell them they were gifted tennis players and really didn't need much coaching.

A coach took over the JV team after I left. She really knew nothing about tennis and just told everyone they were wonderful players. Not only did this ensure discouragement when they lost matches, but it also created a lack of confidence in other areas of their life. Losing was not attributed to a lack of work; it was blamed on their lack of talent and ability. We need to encourage kids who work hard towards the things they want instead of avoiding goals they think they don't have the ability to achieve.

Praising is always difficult to maintain. You set a high bar for your kids, and want to make sure they will achieve great things. But it does no good to praise your children only when they achieve success. It's much better to praise their effort.

SUCCESSIVE APPROXIMATION

Would you like to learn a better way to praise your child into becoming a Results-Focused Mindset superstar? In my graduate school days when I was getting my PhD, I studied under a professor taught by B.F. Skinner, the father of behavior modification. You have probably heard negative things about behavior modification or operant conditioning. You may think it's a matter of putting electrodes in people's heads or giving them treats for strange behavior. But the field has come a long way.

One tenet of operant conditioning is *successive approximation.* Have you ever wondered how animal trainers create such amazing tricks? How does Shamu at SeaWorld jump one hunded feet in the air through a fiery hoop? Do you think the trainers just wait for Shamu to do this and then reward her? No, they've trained her with a series of behaviors approximating the end result. At first they put a hoop on top of the water with a fish inside the hoop as a reward. Then they put a hoop one foot out of the water and wait for Shamu to put her nose through, again receiving the reward. This goes on for months and months: rewarding Shamu for approximating, or getting closer to, the goal. Finally Shamu jumps 100 feet in the air through a fiery hoop to thunderous applause. But this happens only after months of gradually getting closer to the end result.

This is how to develop a Results-Focused Mindset in your kids. First, praise them for spending a few minutes of effort toward the goal. Then praise them for more effort and hard work. After a few days or weeks, continue to praise them for hard work and more achievement, but never for the effort they put in last week. Praise them only for the successively greater amount of effort they put in today. By successively praising people for approximating the goal, you can shape a better mindset.

The truth is, successive approximation can help you behavior-shape any goal. You can develop sales skills in an employee or better communication with an assistant; you can even teach a relative to be on time. Praising people for getting better at something will not only achieve the goal but will help develop a Results-Focused Mindset in the process.

As I mentioned earlier, praising someone's talent is a surefire way to create a fixed mindset. But praising somebody's work is an equally effective way at developing a Results-Focused Mindset. I sarcastically tell some of my tennis friends that they are just too smart. This is usually a response to bragging about a success or about how they were able to get one over on somebody else. But if you really cared about someone's ability to grow, you would never complement who they are. You would only complement their effort and performance.

One Harvard study showed that money is the number one reason why people join a company. This is followed by fun, training, support, and recognition. The fun and training aspectss are especially prized by millennials, who want to increase their value in a future company as well as enjoy the process. I once employed a twenty something fresh out of James Madison University, from which my daughter Stacey had also graduated. This young girl worked for me over the summer and left for Enterprise Rent-a-Car after only three months. When I asked why she left a prestigious consulting company for Enterprise, she said Enterprise was more fun. They had beer parties after work on Friday nights.

What do you think the biggest reason is for an employee to leave a company? Money? Fun? Would you believe recognition? For a nonmillennial, recognition is the biggest reason to stay with a company. But unless you want to develop a fixed-mindset employee who feels superior, makes excuses for setbacks, and has a hard time developing new skills, you need, again, to complement their effort and performance, not who they are.

Here are a few rules that you can use to recognize the people you work and help develop a Results-Focused Mindset. A rule of thumb is praise people at least three times a day. I'm not talking about insincerely giving compliments. I'm talking about praising people for their actual effort. This will create higher morale and will encourage people to look forward to going to work. One of my clients, a mortgage-company owner in Louisiana, pushed back on me when I suggested praising his staff more often. He said, "They don't do anything worth praising." After a week on our next coaching call, he said, "That praising stuff really works. One of my staff came into my office and said I don't know what changed, but the office just feels better. It's more fun."

Here's a three-part process to praising people and helping them develop a Results-Focused Mindset.

1. Praise people in front of other people. This will cause everybody on your team to feel better but also to strive to be the recipient of future praise.

2. Be very specific in your praise. Often my coaching clients will say to a staff person, "Great job." But it's a great job for what? What you

want them to do is replicate the behavior they got praised for. Instead say, "Great job on hitting that deadline for our client. That really meant a lot." The likelihood of that person hitting deadlines in the future increases dramatically.

3. Praise people globally. This means is letting them know how much you appreciate their hard work, and how much you value their effort and dedication.

In short, never praise who the person is, only their behavior. Never say, "You are so smart, we are lucky to have you." Or, "With your talent and experience, we will hit our financial goals forever." This will create a fixed mindset, and your staff will assign blame, diminish your coaching, and lose motivation. But by praising effort, you will create people who look forward to developing their skills and earning praise in the future.

THE SHY MINDSET

Here's a question. Do shy people have a fixed or Results-Focused Mindset?

Psychological researcher Jennifer Beer studied mindsets of both shy and outgoing people. She filmed interactions between these groups and evaluated their methods of communication. She found that fixed-mindset people were more likely to be shy. They were more concerned about being judged, which also made them more self-conscious and anxious. But the surprising part is that while shyness decreased the social interactions of fixed-mindset folks, it didn't measurably harm the communication skills of those with a growth mindset.

This should make sense after we have heard so much about the differences in mindsets. Shy people with a growth mindset look at social interactions as a challenge. When they feel anxious meeting somebody new, they try to overcome their anxiety. The shy people with fixed mindsets also feel nervous, but they are more likely to avoid interpersonal interactions, including talking and eye contact. Once again, the growth-mindset people looked at shyness as a stepping-stone to improvement, while the fixed mindset people try to avoid new relationships.

THE MINDSET OF A WOMAN

There also seems to be gender differences in mindset. Who do you think is more likely to have a fixed mindset: males or females? Who is more likely to have a Results-Focused Mindset? During my seminars, I often ask who takes rejection better: males or females? The answer is that males do. I jokingly say that we are better at rejection because we've had more of it. I say that when I was in college, women I didn't even know would call me on the phone and say, "Don't ask me out!"

A lot of the gender differences in mindset have to do with how girls and boys are raised. Boys are constantly scolded, diminished, and corrected. During seminars, I humorously say that if an overweight male friend comes off an airplane after ten years, his friend might say, "Really packed it on, Bubba." But if an overweight woman after ten years comes off a plane, both male and female friends are likely to say, "That muumuu looks great on you."

This has happened to boys so much that it tends to diminish criticism from others in later life. If a friend says you have no idea how to dress, a male's thought is likely to be, "I don't care, I like this shirt." My wife, Merita, will take a short scan of what I am wearing before we go out. When I hear, "You're not going to wear that, are you?" I know I need to change or hear for the next hour why I shouldn't have worn something. But if she ever asks me how she looks, I automatically say ,"Beautiful." If I don't, she will model the right outfit for the next twenty minutes, with me involved.

Often girls are protected. Parents, teachers, and friends tell them how beautiful, smart, and talented they are. This creates successful women with a fixed mindset. Because they were not harassed the way boys were when they were young, criticism when they are older has a much bigger impact. In one study, successful women were asked about their vulnerabilities. Many were worried that they would be found out. They thought that they really didn't deserve their success. Others, even though they were much more talented and gifted, still had an ongoing level of anxiety.

Most men have learned never to ask if a woman is pregnant. Even if she is in her ninth month and minutes away from going to labor, men fear a woman's response if it turns out that she is not pregnant. Personally I've made this mistake more than once. I'm pretty conversational and often want to chat about the obvious. Most men are smarter than I and never broach the subject. But I've stupidly done it three times, and I hope I never will again.

So if you're a woman, realize that you may have a natural tendency toward a fixed mindset. You may have to work harder than men to stay growth-focused. You may have been raised with people telling you how great you looked and how smart you were. With luck, you only listened to the praise about your hard work and effort—not about your talent and appearance.

DOESN'T TALENT MAKE UP FOR A LACK OF HARD WORK?

One of most common misconceptions about mindset is that natural talent means that you don't require work or effort. Tiger Woods set a course record at Hacienda Country Club in La Habra Heights, California, when he was only seventeen. He was widely regarded as the most talented golfer in history. But he didn't come packaged as a phenomenon. His father put a golf club in Tiger's hands as soon as he could walk. At three years old, he was featured on daytime TV hitting a golf ball in a simulator. No doubt he had talent, but hard work developed that talent and made him a champion.

In 1988, quarterback Ryan Leaf was selected as number two in the NFL draft, right behind two-time Super Bowl champion Peyton Manning. Ryan had every bit as much talent and ability as Manning. But Manning immediately overshadowed him.

Ryan's story is remarkable in the light of mindset. According to a recent Fox Sports report, he was paid $5 million a year, yet he didn't even like to play football. He knew he had amazing talent, but he did not have the passion. He spent two years in the NFL, never putting in the hard work or effort that a player with a Results-Focused Mindset would have. Ryan was gifted, but he wasn't willing to work. There was no passion for developing that talent. Because of a fixed mindset that valued talent and nothing else, he was destined at best to be mediocre.

Ryan started doing drugs heavily and eventually was released from the San Diego Chargers. Two years later, he left football completely. He moved back to his home town in Montana and started to slide downhill. He spend two years in prison for drug offenses. He later said he was grateful he didn't commit suicide.

Ryan now works with released prison convicts and drug offenders, helping them recover and gain a better life. Ryan Leaf found his way. It just wasn't through football.

Carol Dweck has written about baseball player Maury Wills. In the 1950s, the highly motivated Wills had a dream of becoming a major leaguer. But it seemed that a dream was all he had. His hitting wasn't good enough, and the Los Angeles Dodgers sent him to the minor leagues. Forever hopeful, Maury told his friends he'd be back in the majors, playing with Jackie Robinson within two years. Two years became eight and a half years. Eventually Wills was called up to the majors after a shortstop broke his toe. His batting still wasn't good enough, but he was forever positive and focused on becoming a better hitter. He went to his first-base coach for help. They worked many hours a day on top of Wills's regular practice. He studied various pitches and how to predict ball flight as it came off the pitcher's hand. He started to get better. But his real strength came from his ability to steal bases with great speed. The threat of stealing distracted both pitchers and catchers, not only helping teammates to get on base faster, but also winning games. Wills eventually went on to break Ty Cobb's record for stolen bases, a record that had lasted forty-seven years.

It's impossible to have a fixed mindset and continue to improve in the minors for eight and a half years. To have that kind of patience, you need to have a dream and continually work hard. You need to have the faith that you will accomplish your dreams if you put enough effort in.

Think about your career. What if you made $1000 a month for eight years, knowing that your contemporaries were making ten times that much? Could you have been patient? Could you have stuck it out for eight years trying to get your chance? Not many people could. A Results-Focused Mindset is the only way to do it.

Michael Jordan was interviewed on CBS's *Sixty Minutes*. Journalist Steve Kroft reminded him that he had been cut from his high-school basketball team. At the end of the interview, Kroft asked if Jordan would like to play one-on-one. After a ten-point shut out, Kroft asked if Jordan would ever let him win. Jordan said, "Never." Kroft said, "Have you ever lost? Michael said, "Of course." Kroft said, "What did you do?" Jordan replied, "I kept playing till I won." Similarly, the legendary NFL coach Vince Lombardi once said, "We didn't lose the game, we just ran out of time."

Sure, Michael Jordan had great talent. But more remarkable was his work ethic. Not only did he work hard, but kept working until he won. Very few athletes have that kind of dedication or mindset.

THE ARROGANT MINDSET

I've already told the story of how GE bought Kidder, Peabody because of hubris. The GE executives thought they were the smartest people in the room. All the same, Kidder Peabody lost hundreds of millions of dollars for GE.

The Japanese arguably lost World War II because of hubris. After their victories in China and the Philippines and at Pearl Harbor, the Japanese military seemed invincible. Having received intelligence information that the they would be invading Midway Island in the central Pacific, U.S. Admiral Chester W. Nimitz set a trap for Japanese naval commander Admiral Isoroku Yamamoto. The U.S. would ambush the Japanese navy at Midway, trying to take out their four aircraft carriers. It was a huge gamble, risking the rest of the U.S. carrier fleet in one battle. If Nimitz had lost that battle, there would have been nothing holding the Japanese back from invading California and the West Coast.

But the Japanese made a fatal fixed-mindset mistake. They split their eastward forces, sending half the fleet to the Aleutian Islands off Alaska and the other half to Midway. They were so confident that America was no match for the superior Japanese force that they took unnecessary risks. If the Japanese forces hadn't been separated, they could have defeated the U.S. Navy at Midway and possibly won the Pacific.

Hitler made some of the same arrogant, fixed-mindset mistakes. Germany decided to invade Russia in the middle of World War II, taking pressure off of their campaign against Great Britain. If Hitler had focused only on Britain instead of simultaneously invading Russia, he might have won the war in Europe. Then he could have maintained enough strength to conquer Russia. But Hitler had a fixed mindset. He thought that Aryans were superior and the Russians subhuman. Fixed-mindset hubris again changed history.

The Japanese were barbaric in their treatment of Filipinos, Chinese, and Americans all through World War II, especially as they retreated. They even abrogated the Geneva Convention code of civil treatment for prisoners of war. After many mass murders, top Japanese commanders were asked how they could be so brutal. All said that the Japanese were a superior people; the rest of the nations and races were inferior and deserve to be killed. There was also mass murder of POWs by German forces. More than two hundred American GIs were murdered in the Ardennes forest of the Battle of the Bulge. When German officers were asked about their brutality, they said the same thing: Americans were inferior and deserved to be killed.

According to Edward Gibbon's *The Decline and Fall of the Roman Empire*, conquering generals who returned to Rome with plunder and slaves were welcomed with magnificent triumphal processions. But the generals always had a person in the ceremonial chariot whispering, "You are only a man, you are only a man."

So it seems that success can create hubris. Hubris can create a fixed mindset. And that can create failure.

Conclusion

You have learned a lot in this book about why mindset is so important to your success. Mindset is everything. It's how you think and how you perceive the world. Your mindset is a result of your beliefs and experiences. It sets the stage for how you respond to everything.

You have learned also how mindset affects your self-confidence, and how your mindset creates biases that filter information. You have learned about the inward mindset of thinking mainly about yourself and about the more effective outward mindset of working through others to achieve your goals.

You also learned that a fixed mindset sees setbacks and failures as a commentary about a person's abilities and talents. A growth mindset, on the other hand, sees setbacks and failures as stepping-stones to lead to better outcomes later. A growth mindset promises limitless potential, while the fixed mindset causes you to blame and deny.

You learned about how important it is to combine the outward and growth mindsets into one that produces results—a Results-Focused Mindset. You have also learned how to recast how you think about future and past experiences in new ways that support the mindset you want.

You learned how to change your beliefs by changing your memories. Through neurolinguistic programming, you now are able to see, hear, or feel a belief. Now you know how to intensify or dim those representations, which in turn increases your confidence and decreases your anxiety.

You have even learned how to change your emotions in seconds using a resource circle and attachment. We've spent a lot of time discussing meta-patterns, the thought modes you use. If you can change your meta-patterns, you can create a Results-Focused Mindset.

Since goals are much easier to accomplish with the right mindset, you learned how to slice goals into bite-size activities, making them short-, medium-, and long-term. We also learned how to experience the goal instead of just writing it down. The more you can experience the goal as an outcome, the more motivated you will be to achieve it.

You have set goals before and failed to accomplish them, just as New Year's resolutions are rarely kept. So you have learned how to stay committed to your goals by creating a behavioral contract, enforced by using immediate rewards. You learned how to behavior-shape with successive approximation—making small changes that approximate, little by little, the end results you want to achieve.

You have learned how the brain is impacted by your mindset. If you worry, you will create brain pathways that will cause you to worry more. But the more you use a Results-Focused Mindset, the more the brain creates neural freeways that will make it consistently easier to stay positive and focused on the results you want. You have also learned how to change the way you think, using the pattern-interrupt technique, followed by a reward substitution.

You learned why a Results-Focused Mindset is often helped by struggle: the more you challenge yourself, the more mentally and physically sharp you will be. Your Results-Focused Mindset will deteriorate without consistently taking risks. In this section you also learned how great leaders use a Results-Focused Mindset to develop people and negotiate better.

You now also know that your mindset is also important in creating and maintaining great relationships. You can actually create a desire in others to learn and focus on effort through the technique of three-step praise. You even learned how you develop a better mindset in your children, and how one symptom of a fixed mindset can be shyness. We discussed how girls are usually raised in a fixed-mindset environment but how they can grow into a Results-Focused Mindset later.

Lastly, we learned that talent is no substitute for effort. Only those who are able to develop their abilities are able to achieve their outcomes. We've also learned that arrogance and superiority are the opposite of a growth and Results-Focused Mindset.

When I was in college in 1976, I played with an upcoming tennis star dead-set on competing on the international tour. He was a heck of a player, with a blistering serve and never-miss groundstrokes. He was also the most motivated person I had ever met. He narrowly beat me in a three-set match. Afterward, we spent a couple of hours talking about tennis and about our goals for the future. I mentioned a desire to play on the tour for a couple years also. But if that didn't work out, I would go to graduate school to study for my PhD.

I asked this very enthusiastic player what his goals were. He said, "It's very simple. I am going to play on the tour and be number one in the world." He showed me pictures of the Wimbledon trophy, the French Open trophy, as well as trophies from the rest of the grand-slam tournaments. He pulled out letters from other touring pros he had met, wishing him good luck. I had a cherished picture signed by 1960s tennis great Rocket Rod Laver, wishing me good luck on the tour also. But this young budding superstar had a file folder of pictures, letters, and tennis notes, all designed to motivate him.

He went on to become one of the top fifty in the world. I gave up after two years and went to graduate school. Like the Spanish captain Hernán Cortés in 1519, who, upon landing in Veracruz, Mexico, burned his ships to make sure his crew had nowhere to retreat from the Aztecs, this player was completely dedicated and committed to his goal. He had a mindset that would carry him through, no matter how hard he had to work. In his mind, becoming a top touring pro was more a matter of effort and work than talent. I soon learned that mindset is what drives everything.

Mindset impacts your goals, your beliefs, and even your satisfaction. Mindset is where it all starts. You have learned a lot in this book that you can use today. Please make an attempt to apply these techniques for the next three weeks. If you want really want to change to a Results-Focused Mindset, it will take commitment and effort. Of course, now you know that effort is everything.

Printed in the USA
CPSIA information can be obtained
at www.ICGtesting.com
JSHW012029140824
68134JS00033B/2953